ex $18.95

$13

AMERICA
THROUGH BASEBALL

David Q. Voigt

AMERICA
THROUGH BASEBALL

Nelson-Hall nh Chicago

Library of Congress Cataloging in Publication Data

Voigt, David Quentin.
    America through baseball.

    Includes index.
    1.   Baseball—History—United States—Addresses,
essays, lectures.   2.   United States—Social life and
customs.   I.   Title.
GV863.A1V64   1976   796.357'0973   75-20434
ISBN 0-88229-272-2

Manufactured in the United States of America.

TO
my sons, Dave and Mark,
for teaching me that baseball
can also be a fountain of youth.

Contents

Preface

America Through Baseball is a spinoff from a variety of insights resulting from my experience in writing a two-volume narrative history of major league baseball. Having acquired by this work a broad and sweeping knowledge of the game, I turned to particular applications of baseball history mirroring and reflecting larger currents of American social and cultural history. In short, I came to appreciate how a sport like American baseball can be studied as a meaningful cultural institution—much like politics, economics, family life, etc.—and mirror of American life and times. I think that this is the message behind the burgeoning movement toward courses in sociology and history of sports now offered by many colleges. Sports like baseball have always interested and held the attention of Americans; yet too long they have been neglected as frivolous by American academicians. The social and cultural history movement, as well as the expansion of American sociology, gives evidence of the growing recognition of the importance of sport.

In writing this book, I took note of several connections between baseball events and significant trends in American society. Individually several of these insights became subjects of articles I wrote for scholarly journals or addresses I delivered before conventions of historians and sociologists. While pleased at the reception these efforts received, I became more intrigued by the kind of pattern that my efforts presented in their totality.

The four sections in this book of essays display the pattern and, I believe, point toward new directions for students of sport to pursue. The first section, "The Big Picture," shows in broad strokes how the history of baseball mirrors key trends in American social life and embellishes these. The second section, "Saving Myths of American Baseball," shows the sport mirroring some of the most sacred myths of our society, elaborating upon them and often exposing their poverty.

A third section, "Baseball—Mirror of American Life," carries a set of essays showing the sport to be reflecting such basic American ideas as American nationalism, "the mission of America," the American dilemma of racism, and the rising unionization ethic embraced by American workers. And the final section, "American Baseball in a Changing Society," explores ongoing patterns of change in the nation. The latter essays in particular explore the changing nature of American hero worship and the shaping impact of new dimensions of communications media upon American behavior.

I hope that the areas explored in this book may point the way for a continuing serious study of sport by historians, social scientists, and aficionados.

This book is addressed to my colleagues in social science and to sports buffs. May both tribes increase, especially the former for having so long borne the burden of academic snobbery. But the climate is changing. The latest "New History" movement is lending respectability to the serious study of sport and groups of sports students are springing up in academia. Recently the American Historical Association and the American Sociological Association each added sections in sports studies to their annual meeting program. And last year a band of anthropologists organized the Association for the Anthropological Study of Play. Even more hopeful is the appearance of courses in the study of sport in general, and here and there on American baseball in particular.

Today organizations for the study of sport are thriving lustily. Five years ago the Popular Culture Association stood almost alone in offering a haven for sports students. Now there is the North American Society for the Study of Sports History, the International Symposium for the Sociology of Sport, and the Society for American Baseball Research (SABR), which shelters scholars and laymen together.

As current president of SABR, I hope that society's example of bridging the gap between academics and laymen will inspire similar organizations to do likewise. As curing is too important to leave only to doctors or soul-saving to clergy alone, likewise sport is too much for mere academics!

BALL 1

The big picture

That established sports of a society mirror the culture of that society has long been recognized by students of human nature, but scant effort has been expended to display this reflection. The central theme of the following essay, "America Through Baseball," is the presence of sport in society and society's presence in the sport of major league baseball. The changing world view of Americans and the changing values, ethics, and lifeways of the past century of American history are sketched in broad strokes.

1

America through baseball

"He who would know the heart and mind of America had better learn baseball." From a serious student of ideas, Jacques Barzun, this statement serves both as justification and apology for my interpreting American culture through baseball. But why should I apologize for such an undertaking? Perhaps because of the soul-destroying, humanistic fallacy dictating that the serious study of a culture follows well-trodden roads—preferably trends in esthetics, philosophy, economics, or politics. To take the path of sports is to be off the track. And yet many intellectuals are interested in baseball. As one reviewer put it: "They keep turning their interest over like a curious object, inspecting it from all sides, trying to figure out some way to *analyze* it." An interesting paradox, the reviewer called it "a part of their bewilderment at being Americans." [1]

For now at least the student of baseball must shoulder the thinly disguised contempt of his colleagues. Of course, his lot is lighter than that of the late Alfred Kinsey, whose researches into American sex behavior carried his reputation to extremes of fame and infamy. Kinsey's defensive reaction was to bury himself in research at his institute at Indiana

University, where his long hours of labor prompted his wife to quip: "I never see Alfred now that he's taken up sex!" He overworked, and his untimely death suggests the extreme price sometimes paid by a scholarly maverick.

Happily there are indications that the world of knowledge is at last recognizing that to know a civilization is to probe all aspects of its behavior. Today, if Everett Hale's forlorn hero, Philip Nolan, were to ask on his death-bed, "Tell me about America," we would hardly know where to begin. A human paleontologist gives a rundown on the fossil record of early man in America; an archeologist like Paul Mangelsdorf might discourse on the significance of the domestication of corn; a student of language like Eric Partridge or Ashley Montagu might review the history of American slang and swearing; a feminist like Betty Friedan might celebrate the rising power of American women; a black man might expound on the long oppression of blacks and their coming liberation; and a sociologist of sex might cite the transition toward a pattern of "permissiveness with affection" in sex relations. Today all these approaches compete with traditional replies which stressed America's military, political, economic, literary, or philosophical transformation. Such insights into American behavior suggest that at last we are disenthralled from singleminded answers to "What is an American?"

Today, hundreds of institutions, large and small, are under scholarly scrutiny as we begin to understand that reflections of American life can be glimpsed wherever groups of Americans share an activity. And certainly American baseball is not the least of these shared activities. A century old in 1971, major league baseball's history affords insights aplenty to Crèvecoeur's haunting question, "Who is this new man, this American?"

THE RISE OF MAJOR LEAGUE BASEBALL

A nineteenth century field sport evolving out of children's bat and ball games, American baseball appeared as an exclusive team sport for urban gentlemen in Massachusetts and New York. For a time aristocratic clubs like the New York Knickerbockers tried to monopolize the game as a gentlemen's pastime in much the same way as the Marylebone Club dominated English cricket. But with new baseball teams springing up in other urban centers, surging public interest speeded the proletarization of the game. By 1860 spectators were paying to see games, opening the door to commercialism. At the same time intense competition among clubs led to paying good players so that the sport quickly evolved into a commercialized spectacle. By 1869 control of the game's development was in the hands of professional interests. For a brief period professional players controlled big time baseball, but owners moved against the rickety players' league in 1876, replaced it with the National League of Professional Baseball *Clubs*, and established control over the major league game. Shorn of power, the players soon lost their next best weapon, their right to quit a club and offer their services to another. Fully aware of the divisive consequences of such freedom, the owners invoked the reserve clause and made it a part of player contracts.

To establish control over all phases of commercial baseball, major league owners brought the minor leagues under their control and established a system of territorial rights protecting each owner. Meanwhile at annual meetings owners determined the changing rules of play, the shifting of franchises, and the hiring and firing of umpires and other officials.

Sometimes powerful officials challenged owners' power, but even men like Ban Johnson and Judge Kenesaw M. Landis had to face the fact of ultimate owner power. Fully operational by 1880, owner control was challenged by rival major leagues. Most such threats were beaten or bought off by the National League, but the briefly successful American Association and the permanently successful American League were brought under the National League umbrella of owner control. Jointly formed National Agreements testified to the

5

wedding of common owner interests despite their rival league affiliations.

In the aftermath of the baseball wars of the nineteenth century the owners came to know the wisdom of banding together. In 1890 the players revolted and formed their own major league, but despite suffering heavy losses, the owners of the National League and American Association joined forces to beat off the threat. When the National League and American Association quarreled over the division of the spoils, the National League owners crushed their old allies by absorbing four Association teams into the National League. Hence, from 1892 to 1901 the National League owners monopolized major league ball. But when their single twelve-club "big league" failed to prosper, the challenging American League was awarded big league status. In 1903 President Ban Johnson of the American League joined with the National and a new National Agreement was signed. Under its terms two major leagues coexisted and the annual champions of each league were to meet each October in a "World Series" to decide the mythical world championship.

This last accommodation was so successful that for half a century thereafter not a single franchise shift took place in either major league. A most unusual period of stability, it fixed itself in the public mind, giving the impression of changelessness in American baseball. During the age great teams rose to dynastic heights and fell, and a joint commission form of control was replaced by a single commissioner with powers more mythical than real. As always the owners retained control. Today, amid a plastic age of shifting franchises, expanding leagues, and bewildered fans, this fact of power remains constant.[2]

IMAGES OF AMERICA IN BASEBALL—
DYNAMIC INDIVIDUALISM

What I have sketched of baseball's political history is familiar to most fans. Always popular, major league baseball adjusted its playing style often enough to maintain its popularity. I maintain that such changes in major league baseball's style of play, cast of characters, promotion policies, along with other aspects, both mirror and reflect broader changes in American character. Although that will-o'-the-wisp called national character is a difficult idea to pin down anywhere, in pluralistic America the quest is maddening. At once individual and social in manifestation, always contradictory and polytypic in its traits, everchanging and never stable, the American character admits no permanent standards of normality or deviance. This dynamic portrait of American life is mirrored in major league baseball. Indeed, if major league owners have learned anything after a century of promotion, it is that to survive and to profit in a changing world one must keep pace with changes in other institutions. This major league baseball has done; often muddlingly to be sure, but well enough to sustain public interest. In these patterns of adjustment and in their shaping processes, one can see broader patterns of changing behavior, typical of American life in general.

Certainly one dominating value of our social history has been our celebration of individualism. A driving American theme, this faith in the free individual spurs each of us to try to become all that we can be. "To be somebody," to find our identity, and to validate our individualism is a driving theme of Western nations, but it is not a universal idea. In China, for example, anthropologist Francis K. Hsu describes a "jen" model of personality development which works to subordinate individualism to familism. Thus the family group rather than the individual is the unit of achievement, and one gains one's personal ego enhancement as a reflection of the prestige that accrues to the family unit.[3]

Americans, of course, have long insisted that the individual is the basic unit in society. By pursuing this act of faith, we follow a psychology of individuality. A major emphasis in the science of psychology, this school of personality theory dominates American psychology.[4]

The behavior of major league players and their fans reflects our dominant theme of individualism. It is mirrored in the very first stage of major league baseball development. The "gentlemen's era," a stage lasting roughly from 1850 to 1876, was characterized by control of the organized game resting in the hands of aristocratic clubs, organized by aspiring "gentlemen" seeking to validate their claims to high social status. During the 1850s the most aristocratic of clubs was the Knickerbocker Club of New York. In 1845 one of its members designed the familiar diamond-shaped infield with bases set forty-five feet apart. Along with this innovation went a widely imitated set of playing rules and a code of gentlemanly conduct. Above all, the Knickerbockers sought to insure the game's remaining in the hands of gentlemen like themselves, but they failed. For one reason, like most Americans, they had no clear understanding of who or what was a gentleman.[5] For another, like most of their rival clubs, they wanted to win. Thus, the ethic of successful competition which returned cash and glory for outstanding individual performances speeded the proletarization of American baseball.

By 1860 most clubs recruited, and many paid cash to those outstanding players whose social status lagged behind their playing skill. Upgraded and rewarded for their individual performances, stars like Arthur Cummings, James Creighton, Al Reach, and Joe Start emerged as popular idols. By the 1860s their exploits lured fans who willingly paid to see their heroes in action. And as competition heightened among clubs, more spectators came, making the profit potential in baseball attractive to investors. But during the 1860s the real winners were the star players. Popular demand for news of their deeds stimulated baseball journalism and at the parks player picture sales flourished. Thus, the decade of the 1870s saw the emergence of the baseball writer. The ability of such men to sell newspapers was quickly grasped by publishers of great metropolitan dailies and by sporting journal editors like Frank Queen of the *New York Clipper*.

Notwithstanding the interruption by five years of Civil

War, the commercialization and professionalization of American baseball advanced so rapidly in the early 1870s as to admit the first major league. In 1871 the leading clubs and players organized the National Association of Professional Base Ball Players, thus opening a new career field for athletically endowed youths with ambitions "to be somebody." From 1871 till this day, the professional ethic dominated baseball, and the best professional players measured their skill and worth by their salaries. Of course, the dominance of the professional player ended the heyday of the gentlemen amateurs. Rudely bypassed, shunted aside by professionals, some gentlemen players continued to play. But more contented themselves with their financial support of professional teams, and most would-be gentlemen turned to other leisure or athletic outlets in hopes of validating their social worth.

In passing the gentlemen's era left an indelible mark on American baseball. From 1871 until this day it is a rare club owner who depends on his baseball earnings for his livelihood. Usually, an owner has some outside source of income so that his baseball involvement is a secondary business venture. For many owners baseball investment is a device for ego enhancement or conspicuous display. While some businessmen purchase strings of racehorses to validate their sporting claims, others find baseball promotion similarly useful.

As a high level status symbol baseball promotion owes much of its attractiveness to free newspaper publicity. In the 1890s when the twelve-club National League monopolized major league baseball, this fact was most evident. In that decade when Americans were fascinated by the deeds of businessmen and industrialists, baseball owners styled themselves as "magnates." Some, like Frank de Hass Robison, took their promotion so seriously as to form a "syndicate" of major league teams. As owner of two big league teams, Robison was in competition with himself, which carried the robber baron bit rather far. By the end of the decade, muckraking sportswriters caught up with such magnates and forced an end to their practice. The same reformers also turned the spotlight

9

of publicity onto the players and away from the owners so that owners never regained the publicity and notoriety that was theirs in the 1890s.[6]

The persistence of the gentleman-sportsman-owner is evidenced in the career of Tom Yawkey of the Boston Red Sox and the careers of men like the late Jacob Ruppert of the New York Yankees and August Busch of the St. Louis Cardinals. As brewery owners this pair gained most of their income outside the game, but baseball certainly advertised their foamy product. At the same time such men gained social esteem that might not have come their way had they limited themselves solely to beer. Only recently, in fact, has beer consumption become respectable in middle-class America, and long lasting taboos, combined with a century old tradition linking baseball promotion with breweries, have for the most part made the major league game seem sinful to many middle-class Americans.

A large percentage of today's income of baseball owners comes from television contracts. By exposing the owner and the team to a wider public, the new medium has enhanced the owner's public image. Thus, in ever-changing pattern the status of gentleman-owner continues to offer baseball investors hope that their investment might reap a special kind of award—public recognition of their unique individualism.

Meanwhile players found baseball to be a promising road to individual recognition. Perhaps as much as any institution, American baseball kept alive Horatio Alger's myth that a hungry, rural-raised, poor boy could win middle-class respectability through persistence, courage, and hard work. Until recently, major league salaries always compared favorably with middle range incomes in business or in the professions. And as Babe Ruth proved in the late 1920s, a superstar might command more money than the American President, testifying to America's becoming a nation of celebrity watchers. Ruth's high position in the pantheon of American celebrities shows how high a peak a driven young man might scale.

For more than a century now the siren call of a big league

career has spurred young hopefuls. In the nineteenth century, Irish-American lads sought an escape from discrimination by what they hoped would be the quick baseball road to cash and glory. For inspiration they looked to heroes like Mike Kelly, Ed Delahanty, or Jim O'Rourke, a trio of hard-hitting superstars. Meanwhile children of other immigrant groups nursed similar dreams. In the 1870s Lipman Pike emerged as a Jewish star, and in the 1890s German-American stars like Ted Breitenstein and infielder "Honus" Wagner inspired by their examples. Soon after, Italian-American lads looked to the careers of such stars as "Ping" Bodie (whose real name was Francesco Pezzola), Tony Lazzeri, and Joe Di Maggio; Polish-American boys identified first with the Coveleskie brothers, Al Simmons (nee Syzmanski), and later with Stan Musial; Russo-American youths looked to Lou Novikoff and Czech-Americans to Elmer Valo.

THE MYTH OF THE MELTING POT

The brilliant success stories of such a variety of hyphenated Americans kept the myth of the American melting pot alive in baseball. Moreover, the success of such players mirrored the processes of invasion and succession which students of immigration advanced in support of the myth. Yet, if the game seemingly supports the myth of the melting pot by its acceptance of diverse ethnic Americans, the game's inability to deal equally with black Americans exposes some of the naivete in the myth. Although a few blacks, like the Walker brothers, who played briefly in the majors in the 1880s, are exceptions, baseball's doors clanged shut in the 1890s at the very time the caste barrier of Jim Crow was excluding blacks from participating in other social institutions.

In truth major league baseball was one of the last professions to lay aside its Jim Crow practices. Before major league baseball admitted its first black player in 1947, blacks already had won acceptance in war industries, military service, and in other professional sports. Yet the major league owners remained tremulous. In 1946 when Branch Rickey moved to prepare Jackie Robinson for his Dodger debut, Robinson was obliged to undergo a process of "niggerization." Warned to curb his temper and to submit silently to racist epithets, Robinson was being asked to play the role of cooperative Negro *par excellence*. In today's parlance, he had to make like an Uncle Tom. Granted that Rickey showed moral courage in bucking his more bigoted colleagues, threatening at one point to expose his colleagues for daring to invoke a "gentleman's agreement" aimed at barring further racial integration in baseball.[7] Yet if today there are more black faces in big league lineups, it is because black players supply more of the available talent. Even so, they must be better than average players to make the majors.[8] This because major league baseball today still follows the rule of the tipping point—an assumption that more than a handful of blacks might destroy the balance of an integrated institution, in this case threatening major league baseball with a possible black flood. Among baseball owners this myth is so well entrenched as to rival the fears of realtors or school superintendents. Even stronger among minor league owners, the myth recently was expressed to a reporter by President Sam Smith of the Southern League: "Let's face it, there are folks down here who just don't want their kids growing up to admire a Negro ballplayer even if he's Willie Mays or Hank Aaron."[9]

The same squeamish treatment of socially defined undesirables was reflected in the recent ballpark building boom in the majors. Because such ballparks as Chicago's Comiskey Park and Yankee Stadium in New York are thought to be liabilities inasmuch as their immediate neighborhoods have turned predominately black, most new parks like Candlestick Park in San Francisco, Shea Stadium in New York, and the Astrodome in Houston all huddle close to suburban white refuges. There they testify to the cutting edge of America's latest trend in urban growth. While such examples can be used to fault baseball men for a lack of moral courage, it is fairer to portray these examples as part of the complex American character which resists integration and continues to perceive black Americans to be less than human.

Yet the winds of change blow unceasingly, and if America is exposed as a melting pot society that never melts but only marinates, one must prepare to meet other social problems that swirl around our racial dilemma. Because black players are highly "visible," they have not been equally welcomed into the pantheon of national celebrities. Indeed, a star of the magnitude of Hank Aaron, who in 1974 topped Babe Ruth's lifetime mark of 714 homers, found himself the recipient of angry hate mail for doing so. Yet even as the status of blacks in baseball continues to be ambivalent, other ethnic peoples press for recognition. Since World War II, Puerto Rican players along with other Latin-Americans are crowding into major league lineups. Difficult to type racially or ethnically, their presence bewilders fans who are therefore less inclined to identify with their heroics than they were with white hyphenates of earlier eras. The future portends the possibility of more Latin-Americans and Orientals in baseball. Moreover, American women, whose lowly status has sometimes been compared with that of blacks, are pressing for active jobs in baseball. Recently a well qualified umpire, Mrs. Bernice Gara, sued Organized Baseball for the right to perform in the profession, and she won. But after a single outing before a largely curious and hostile minor league assemblage, she retired, claiming to have made her point. Thus, baseball reflects the burgeoning feminist movement.[10]

THE BASEBALL PLAYER AS FOLK HERO

Such trends as these mirror a society whose people are groping for a new social and cultural equilibrium. In a world made small by communications expansion, national boundaries become less restrictive. Indeed, in such a churned up society many people find nationalistic symbols to be less meaningful. Some demand that our society not only mouth platitudes such as equality and justice for all, but also practice them. While baseball as a social institution is more in the baggage train than in the vanguard of such causes, its study offers reflections of such vital movements.

Certainly the changing attitudes of major league players toward their employers reflects the passing of the Horatio Alger myth. In the past aspiring players willingly endured merciless hazings from veteran players, an ordeal so brutal as to goad the young Ty Cobb into bruising fights and into a frantic desire to overcome opposition. As an example of determination conquering adversity Cobb stands alone, but many lesser heroes paid a high emotional price to play major league baseball. For many, success meant deferring marriage, practicing endlessly, sweating out contract offers from devious owners, accepting insults, and worrying about the inevitable pink slip that could end a career on the briefest of notice. Even when established, a player still had to endure the psychology of slumps along with normal fears of being injured, replaced, traded, or reduced in salary.

Not surprisingly many failed. In 1907 Jameson Harper enthusiastically welcomed a tryout with the Detroit Tigers and arrived in camp with a suitcase labeled "Jameson Harper, Ballplayer." This dreadful mistake exposed him to merciless heckling. On the field he was barred from batting practice. At the hotel, he lost out in the grab for food served country-style. And asleep one night, he awoke to see what appeared to be playing cards walking across the floor of his room. Horrified, he discovered it to be another prank; each card was glued to the back of a large cockroach. Although humorous to some, Harper considered it tragic. He never made the grade, nor did his name appear in a big league box score.[11]

Because rewards in baseball long exceeded what one might make in industry, players in the past accepted such treatment. And except for tough initiations, all other fears, including the fear of injury, were accepted as typical of the lot of most workers anywhere. And if players lacked tenure or pension rights, they could find few workers elsewhere who enjoyed them.

That modern players will not tolerate such a life is natural enough, since few workers in unionized industries or professionals will either. Thus, the passing of the driven, hungry ballplayer reflects the passing of the same type of American worker. And like workers who now expect more money for less energy expended, baseball players expect the same. To label modern players "sissies" only indicts our modern society which teaches them what to expect. And as it is useless to appeal to modern workers on the bases of loyalty, duty, honor, and the joy of hard work, it is not to be expected that ballplayers will buy such a message.

With today's highest salaries going to college graduates, ballplayers also want to further their education. This trend now forces baseball recruiters to look to colleges for new talent. And because one's college degree promises a well paying job, a middle-class boy is less willing to sacrifice to further a chancy athletic career. Today many young men might give the minor leagues a try, but if promotions are not quickly forthcoming, they move to other careers.

More money-conscious and more security-conscious than ever before, ballplayers are also less glory-conscious. Perhaps better educations make many cynical of the adulation of the fans or sportswriters. This case was well stated by that highly literate expitcher, Jim Brosnan, when he wrote: "Ballplayers resent being scapegoats, symbols, and story material rather than normal men with a little extra athletic talent. Some even claim that ballplayers are human." [12] Earlier, the great outfielder Ted Williams expressed similar sentiments. Lacking Brosnan's literary acumen, Williams (more like Genghis Cohn in Romaine Gary's novel who "mooned" his Nazi murderers) used the best weapon he had by refusing to tip his hat to fans, and by contemptuously spitting toward hostile sportswriters or shocking them with an obscene finger gesture.

While some conservative alarmists see the death of major

league baseball in these trends, realistically they only mirror similar trends in society at large. Today, many Americans are suspicious of gilded heroes and wicked villains; rigid standards of right or wrong, proper and improper, seem passé. In our increasingly plastic society, we seem in the main to want to be left alone, and we are more tolerant of one's right to "do his own thing," within greatly expanded limits of propriety. Thus, if ballplayers object to being cast in old hero molds, they reflect the popular suspicion of such roles. In baseball today, antiheroes like the ungovernable Alex Johnson or Joe Pepitone have enthusiastic followings similar to those portrayed by the offbeat hero of the film, *The Graduate.*

Like the recent toppling of St. Nicholas, St. Valentine, and St. Christopher from the pantheon of historically certified saints, the decline of the superhero in American baseball further reflects the game's fall from popular interest. Yet the game has not lost fans; far from it. Radio, television, and new stadia have widened the game's appeal putting it far beyond any previous era of attention. Nevertheless, baseball can no longer claim to be America's national game, if indeed it ever was. Instead, the game is one of a flock of popular, commercialized outdoor spectacles, in company with professional football (currently the fairest) and horseracing (traditionally the most popular).

THE LEISURE ETHIC

The growing plenitude of spectator sports now offered to American consumers is a reflected trend. But the expanding sports industry is only a part of America's leisure revolution, the chief characteristic of which is the embracement of a "fun ethic" by a majority of people. To have fun like the "Clairol blonde," to enjoy life in a "once around living world," "to live a little," to be part of a swinging Pepsi generation are all expressions of the fun ethic. In pursuing fun, Americans face a bewildering smorgasbord of choices, with new ones constantly emerging. Not surprisingly, baseball cannot lead the list because no single fun activity leads. As popular tastes are ever reshaped and manipulated by advertising media, baseball men join forces with the manipulators. To lure fans, owners now offer more than a game. Today, music, trick cartoon scoreboards, fireworks, giveaways (including bat days, ball days, helmet days, batting glove days) are all used. All these and more are part of the baseball spectacle. Such frenzied promotional activity suggests that the pursuit of fun is becoming a secular American religion. If true, major league baseball plays a minor role in the new fun morality. Far from shaping the new faith of fun, baseball merely adapts to it.

American baseball also mirrors the drama of the surging fun ethic invading the remaining outposts of entrenched puritanism in organized religion. Not that Americans have abandoned supernaturalism as a result, nor has organized religion lost its hold. Reflected is a declining influence of churches on public behavior and the loss of organized religion's ability to maintain religious-based rules of propriety.

Reflected in the history of major league baseball is the long, losing struggle of religious moralizers against their secular opposition. In baseball the struggle centered around the right to play Sunday baseball and to sell beer or liquor at the parks. A long war, it was marked by advances, retreats, and countermarches on both sides. In the 1880s Sunday baseball was entrenched in the Western cities of the American Association, while the National League sanctimoniously supported the Sabbatarian position. With the collapse of the Association in 1892, some of its franchises joined the expanded National League and the battle for Sunday ball entered a new phase. Reeling under Sabbatarian attacks, baseball gave ground until 1902 saw Sunday games played only in Chicago, St. Louis, and Cincinnati. Elsewhere local and state laws banned such games, often on the pretext of insuring peace and quiet.

But because statistics bore out the profits from Sunday games, baseball owners stiffened their resolve. Then when the "social gospel" movement in American religion took up the

rights of workingmen to Sunday leisure, baseball men piously
jumped on the bandwagon. In the battle of rhetoric over the
pros and cons of Sunday ball, a telling blow was struck by
William Kirk in his poem, "Sunday Baseball":

> The East Side Terrors were playing the Slashers,
>   Piling up hits, assists and errors.
> Far from their stuffy tenement homes,
>   That cluster thicker than honeycombs.
> They ran the bases neath shady trees,
>   And were cooled by the Hudson's gentle breeze.
>
> Mrs. Hamilton Marshall-Gray,
>   Coming from church, chanced to drive that way.
> She saw the frolicking urchins there,
>   Their shrill cries splitting the Sabbath air.
> "Mercy!" she muttered, "this must stop!"
>   And promptly proceeded to call a cop,
> And the cop swooped down on the luckless boys,
>   Stopping their frivolous Sunday joys. . . .
>
> The Terrors and Slashers, side by side,
>   Started their stifling Subway ride,
> Down through the city, ever down,
>   To the warping walls of Tenement Town.
> Reaching their homes, the troublesome tots,
>   Crept away to their shabby cots.
> They thought of the far off West Side trees,
>   And the cool green grass, and the gentle breeze,
> And how they had played their baseball game,
>   Till the beautiful Christian lady came.

Armageddon came in 1918 and ended with the rout of the
New York Sabbatarians. With Al Smith's gubernatorial victory tied partly to the support of Sunday baseball and with
James Walker masterminding the enabling bill through the
legislature, Sunday games came to New York. Elsewhere
Sabbatarian pockets of resistance held out, but Boston was
lost in 1929, and Pittsburgh and Philadelphia conceded limited Sunday ball in 1933.[13]

Since secularism provided its own pantheon of celebrity

gods, one could hardly say theirs was a godless victory. More human than divine, these gods rose and fell with rapidity, being ever at the summons of popular worshippers. But the years immediately following the advent of Sunday ball in New York saw the rise of baseball's greatest god. Greater than "King" Kelly of the 1880s or Ty Cobb of the early 1900s, Babe Ruth attracted worshippers as none before or since. Today, because of competition from other god mills, such as rival professional sports, the movies, or television, it is unlikely that baseball will again produce a god of such power. Lately baseball divinities flash by like meteors, burning out after brief heroic flashings. Thus, the recent rise and fall of Denny McLain or Dale Long (remember him?) or Roger Maris or Reggie Jackson, all show the transitory quality of current baseball gods. Thus does baseball mirror the fate of present day heroes, villains, and fools. For ours is truly an age of "situational celebrities," all packaged, sold, and quickly consumed.

Meanwhile the pampering of baseball fans with sideshows, air conditioning, and a variety of eatables testifies to the power of the American comfort ethic. By no means a new trend, Americans always seemed to have longed for physical comfort. In the early history of major league baseball the national quest for comfort was reflected at the ball parks. In the gentlemen's era, shrewd promoters allowed the well-heeled to watch games while sitting in their carriages. At the same time sun-sheltered pavilions were available at a price. In time bicyclists were accommodated as motorists would be a decade later. And the great park building boom of 1909–13 located baseball parks with an eye for access to public transportation. Most recently the trend is to locate the new super-parks within range of suburban motorists.

Inside a park the public demand for sun-sheltered seats was early recognized and met. If at first promoters catered to menfolks, the more imaginative sensed that comfortable accommodations for women would eventually attract more men. Thus did Chris von der Ahe, president of the St. Louis

Browns in the 1880s, announce his addition of ladies' toilets—
"a necessity in all well ordered grounds." He also threw in
sideshows aplenty at his Sportsman's Park. Included were
fireworks displays, dog races, and beer and liquor stands.
Elsewhere the liquor might be missing, but by the 1890s most
promoters were engaging Harry Stevens, the famous con-
cessionaire, to provide tasty foods, including that baseball
favorite—the hotdog. Today, concessionaires offer a vast variety of eatables, all neatly wrapped to assuage the fears of
a microbephobic fandom. And since a well-fed society is apt
to be well-proportioned in the buttocks, most promoters
heeded the advice of St. Louis fans, in a 1945 response to
questionnaires, on what fans wanted to have in a new park.
Responses were uniformly comfort oriented, ranging from re-
quests for wider seats, glass pillars, and more music. Some of
these features are now familiar parts of modern ballpark ecol-
ogy, and domed air conditioned structures are no longer a
baseball architectural dream.

Accompanying the comfort ethic is a marriage ethic which
has made Americans the most wedlocked people in world
history. In accommodating baseball promotion to this trend,
promoters early catered to women. At first, separate sections
were provided, but soon women invaded all sections of a park,
forcing Manager Harry Wright in the 1890s to wage his losing
battle against cursing males at the Phillies' park.[14] Over
the years this verbal expression of male fellowship, or "bond-
ing behavior" as anthropologists call it, offended less, so that
swearing today is a prerogative of both sexes. Hence, a far
greater challenge was that of adapting baseball to meet the
tastes of dating couples—a challenge met partly by increasing
the number of night games. By World War II baseball had
become a popular outlet for dating couples, one of the few exceptions to Lewis Mumford's complaint that modern cities
"are ill-designed for love." It was not always easy; in Brooklyn promoters once announced engagements during lulls in
the action, but once committed a *faux pas* by announcing the
impending birth of a child. To the unmarried father it was a

shattering surprise: "I didn't even know she was pregnant!"
And since so much marriage leads to swarms of children, promoters now meet the togetherness ethic by offering special
giveaways to youngsters.

Today's popular notion that an unmarried adult must
surely be psychologically maladjusted shows up in the lifestyles of modern ballplayers. In times past married players
were exceptional. Not only was one subjected to extra kidding, but often his married activity was defined as a threat
to team success. In 1889, for example, the married members
of the Brooklyn "Bridegrooms" (it had a half dozen newlyweds in its ranks) voluntarily left their conjugal couches
until after the pennant was clinched. For the next half century
baseball customarily fielded more bachelors than bridegrooms. Often the bachelors lived lonely, celibate lives,
brightened occasionally by encounters with "Baseball Sadies,"
as diamond camp followers were called. Sometimes such encounters ended tragically as in the case of Chick Stahl. Early
in this century he killed himself after a blackmail threat. A
later case, Eddie Waitkus, was shot and wounded by a lovecrazed fan. Today most players are married and owners have
learned to accommodate wives and children even though it
complicates the problem of player morale. Sometimes, as in
the recent episode involving Yankee pitchers Fritz Peterson
and Mike Kekich in an alleged "wife swapping" incident,
baseball leaders worried over the consequences for the game's
"image." Public morality notwithstanding, the interests of
married players are a major factor in travel schedules, player
trades, and spring training. But again baseball's problem is
merely a reflection of a similar problem facing employers
everywhere.

THE UNION ETHIC

The hope of sheltering one's self and family from employer
caprice has prompted many Americans to embrace a union
ethic. As sociologist Robert S. Lynd once observed: "We live

in an era in which only organization counts—values and causes without organizational backing were never so impotent." A succinct description of the union ethic, its influence has driven Americans to join pressure groups in order to get their share of life's goodies. With union backing, workers are able to hold "clout" over employers, and models of union organization have been successfully wielded by professionals, feminists, and blacks.

In baseball the union ethic is mirrored in present day player organizations. Back in 1890 players banded together to form their own major league in an unsuccessful bid to oppose an owner plan to reduce salaries. Since then, players sporadically tried to unionize, their ventures reflecting the up and down pattern of union successes in the economy at large. And like union successes elsewhere, the present day player association gained its greatest victories in prosperous times. American labor history shows most unions becoming entrenched only after 1930, but American baseball's union movement waited even longer for success. Such a lag leads one to question major league baseball's reliability as a social mirror, but confidence is restored when one remembers that players differ from industrial or craft workers. Forced to negotiate contracts as an individual, a player is judged by his most recent performance. In setting pay standards, the brightest stars set the pace and ordinaries are paid further down the yardstick. On the other hand players share many problems with other workers, including retirement. In the case of a baseball player this is a much more poignant problem, since forced retirement comes early in life

Such insecurity echoes prevailing American worker yearnings for job protection. In baseball this intense fear was partly assuaged by pension right victories. Today most players belong to the powerful Major League Baseball Players Association, an organization comparable to white-collar unions. In seeking collective bargaining, players now use strikes and boycotts as weapons. So far the most impressive achievement of this organization has been the securing of pension rights whereby a player with as few as five years' tenure can be paid. More recently, the Association has bargained for more money from television contracts, which is to be shared by the pension fund. Also there is talk of bringing minor leaguers into the pension fold.

Of course, America's embracing the union ethic is but one example of our ongoing modification of the free enterprise credo. Trends like the ever increasing specialization of workers, the easing of toil by ever ingenious machinery, and the increasing role of government in business regulation are economics mirrored in American baseball. In baseball the worker as specialist is evidenced in the use of pinch hitters, in diverse relief pitchers, and in the platooning of players. Baseball teams also use a variety of machines including pitching machines, special groundskeeping machinery, artificial turf, jeeps for delivering pitchers, and elaborate scoreboards capable of posting humorous messages and leading community sings in addition to monitoring the game. Meanwhile, like many industries baseball has felt the restraining hand of governmental regulation. Three times since World War II baseball owners have faced Congressional investigators on the lookout for possible antitrust law violations, and threatening to withdraw the umbrella of protection from such suits which was provided by a 1920 Supreme Court decision. Meanwhile local and state governments are involved in baseball operations. Today no single owner can afford to build a park like Yankee Stadium, the last baseball park built wholly on private capital. Now an owner on the lookout for a park must seek state and local subsidies. And transferring a franchise means clearing the way with local, state and national officials.

In other ways American baseball reflects the strengths and weaknesses of American capitalism. Until World War II baseball promoters hewed closely to the ethic of unbridled free enterprise, thereby widening the gap between rich and poor teams. A rich team, like the Yankees, enjoyed the support of the populous area of greater New York. With such support, owner Jacob Ruppert was able to maintain an elaborate scouting system for recruitment and eventually to corner the market on good players. On the other hand, fielding a have-not team like the Phillies forced a penurious owner like Gerald Nugent to run a parasite franchise. For Nugent any profit came from selling potential stars to wealthier clubs, but it denied Phillies fans a contending club or even a comfortable park. Naturally player morale also suffered since players on wealthier teams drew better salaries.

Today the balance has shifted. With television income assured, no owner need sell players, although lately high salaries compel some to unload stars. Moreover, scouts seldom discover promising stars on today's sandlots. With the sandlots a thing of the past, today's recruiting centers on high schools and colleges, and the recent adoption of a common player draft has "socialized" the recruitment of talent. Thus, it is unlikely that a wealthy owner can now buy a pennant. Such a transformation reflects similar trends in American industry and points to the acceptance of practices once called "cartelistic" or "socialistic". In the euphemistic language of a modern era these are called part of the system of "mixed capitalism."[15]

As a mirror reflecting American lifeways, major league baseball shows many trends that are restructuring our American character. And if there is a single lesson to be learned from such gazing, it is that America is today a highly diversified society. So pluralistic, indeed, that no sport may call itself the national game, as, indeed, no individual or group may call itself truly American. To approximate a true American in today's society, one must be flexible, expectant of change, and ready to adjust to it. Certainly this is a message mirrored in American baseball. Its spokesman was the old Cardinal pitcher Jerome "Dizzy" Dean. Asked about the sore arm so soon to end his playing career, Dean's succinct reply was: "It ain't what it used to be, but then, what the hell is?"

NOTES

1. "The New Books," *Harper's,* July 1968.

2. David Quentin Voigt, *American Baseball: From Gentleman's Sport to the Commissioner System* (Norman, Okla.: Univ. of Okla. Press, 1966).

3. Francis K. Hsu, "Psychological Anthropology: An Essential Defect and Its Remedy." Paper read before meeting of American Anthropological Association, Seattle, Nov. 22, 1968.

4. Robert H. Knapp, "The Psychology of Personality." In Bernard Berelson, ed., *The Behavioral Sciences Today* (New York: Basic Books, 1963), pp. 151–64.

5. Voigt, *American Baseball* (1966), pp. 8–13, 35–68.

6. *Ibid.,* pp. 225–41.

7. Stanley Woodward, *Sports Page* (New York: Simon and Schuster, 1949), pp. 82–83, 134.

8. Aaron Rosenblatt, "Negroes in Baseball: The Failure of Success," *Transaction Magazine* (September 1967), pp. 51–53.

9. J. Anthony Lukas, "Down and Out in the Minor Leagues," *Harper's* (June 1968), p. 74.

10. *Sporting News,* July 15, 1972.

11. David Quentin Voigt, *American Baseball: From the Commissioners to Continental Expansion* (Norman, Okla.: Univ. of Okla. Press, 1970), chap. 3.

12. Jim Brosnan, *The Long Season* (New York: Dell, 1961), p. 160.

13. Voigt, *American Baseball* (1970), chap. 4.

14. Voigt, *American Baseball* (1966).

15. *Ibid.,* chaps. 9–11.

BALL 2

Saving myths of American baseball

Man is a myth making animal and myths are among his most basic needs. Myths are used to support all of his social institutions, including American baseball. If a primary task of social science is to disenthrall man from myths that no longer "fit," the student of sports will not lack employment. The following quartet of essays probes some of the myths which baseball officials zealously espouse as essential to the survival of our "national game." The first essay bares the "immaculate conception" myth which makes claims about the origins of the game. In the same vein the second essay challenges the myth that divinely inspired owners, by their 1876 coup, saved the game from the players' anarchical rule. The third essay shows the abiding faith in rational promotion techniques as evidenced in the career of Harry Wright, the "father of professional baseball." And the final essay probes the myth of major league baseball's self-proclaimed purity by reconsidering the celebrated Black Sox scandal.

2

America's first red scare— the Cincinnati Reds of 1869[*]

If the popularity of major league baseball is now eclipsed by the growing popularity of rival sports, at least America's "national game" can claim to be the oldest in its class. In 1969 the clock ticked off the one hundredth year since the first professional team supposedly took the field. As the story goes (and given half a chance any old time aficionado can relate it), the Cincinnati Red Stockings of 1869 took the field as the first professional team. By their ruthless determination, they won eighty-one straight victories, thus demonstrating the efficiency of the new mercenary method of player recruitment. (The actual figure for consecutive victories is in dispute. The figure 81 is from Henry Chadwick, acknowledged as the "father of the game." See *Chadwick's Base Ball Manual, 1871*, pages 46, 111. However, *Beadle's Dime Baseball Player, 1870*, pages 63–64, also edited by Chadwick, gives a total of 88. The counting of informal games is the center of the dispute.) From that point on it was but a step to the birth of the major leagues and a long period of

---

*First published in *Ohio History*, Vol. 78 (Winter, 1969), 13–24.

franchise stability. (This stability has lately been frequently and rudely shattered by franchise shifts and by rumors of more structural upheaval to come.)

The truth is often strained in the telling and often there is a manufactured quality about baseball myths. For example, baseball's birth is wrapped up in a myth packaged by an official commission which met at the turn of this century to inquire into the game's origins. In highly uncritical fashion, the commission took the dubious word of one of its aged members. He claimed that his boyhood chum and lifelong hero, the late Civil War General Abner Doubleday, had "invented" the game one afternoon in 1839. A similar myth of "immaculate conception" is used to explain the sudden appearance of professional baseball in Cincinnati in 1869.[1]

To begin, there is the claim that the 1869 Cincinnati Reds were the first professional players, an interpretation hinging on the meaning of the word "professional." As applied to ballplayers, it usually refers to one's ability to earn a living playing the game. Using this yardstick, the 1869 Reds were far from first. In the early 1860s Al Reach, star infielder for the Philadelphia Athletics, was paid a straight salary for his services, and most prominent teams of his day had at least two salaried stars on hand to back up their amateurs.[2] Moreover, Harry Wright, the father of professional baseball and later player-manager of the 1869 Cincinnati Reds, wrote in his diary of 1866 that the Athletics were also paying $20 a week to three other players. And in 1868 with nonchalant acceptance, sportswriter Henry Chadwick listed the names of ten professionals on the Brooklyn Eckfords.[3]

Nor was the straight salary route the only avenue to baseball professionalism in the formative years. According to the National Association of Base Ball Players a player was a professional if he was given "place or emolument." [4] In the 1860s this qualified quite a few lusty lads under a system which provided "honorary" jobs that called for good pay and almost no work. In the case of the New York Mutuals such jobs were to be found in the Coroner's office; and, in Washington, the Treasury Department was reputed to be "the real birthplace of professional baseball." Elsewhere, in similar fashion, local civic leaders did their part so that their local team might compete in an age of bitter intercity rivalry.[5]

Yet another road to professionalism was the time-honored custom of passing the hat at important games and dividing receipts among stars. This common practice in Washington, Philadelphia, and Brooklyn often brought stars as much as $200 for a day's work. A popular variation of this theme was the benefit game held to honor stars. In 1863 Wright pocketed $29.65 from such an honoring, with some of the money coming from the sale of souvenir tickets with "a picture of a Professional on each." [6]

Not surprisingly, such payoffs evoked criticism from amateur elements who charged that gamblers were contributing to the commercializing process by bribing players to throw games. By 1869 the ugly word "Hippodroming" was widely used to describe games suspected of having been rigged by gamblers. In 1870 the New York Mutuals became a center of controversy when it was rumored that one of their stockholders, William Marcy ("Boss") Tweed, had contributed $7,500 to the team. As one outraged amateur protested at the meeting of the National Association, Tweed "probably got his money back again." [7]

With professional baseball an entrenched reality by 1868, skilled players found themselves in an enviable seller's market, able to get more money from owners by threatening to leave. In blasting such "revolvers" for jumping "without so much as a by your leave," Chadwick demanded restrictions: "Since professional baseball is a business," it should be pursued "honestly and openly and above board." [8]

Partly in response to such demands, but mostly in the interest of team stability and profits, Harry Wright as player-manager of the Red Stockings elected to sign all of his 1869 Reds to full season contracts and to challenge even the best eastern teams. It was not a sudden decision, for the bearded Wright, who had spent most of his life playing, managing, and studying field sports, first as a cricketer and then as a baseball player, knew what he was doing. Sons of a noted cricket professional, Wright and his brother George were ranked among the best ballplayers in America. Moreover, Wright knew where the best men were and was confident of his ability to obtain them.[9]

What amazed Wright's rivals was that a mere western team would dare to actualize such a dream. In the recent past other clubs had taken the grand tour, but they were established eastern teams, like the Washington Nationals or the Brooklyn Eckfords. That a western team might gain prestige from such a venture helped to sell Wright's plan to local backers. Certainly the city of Cincinnati was growing and some leading citizens were anxious for a national identity that would erase Cincinnati's snide reputational epithet of "Porkopolis."

Among the leading boosters of Wright's plan was a twenty-six-year-old lawyer, Aaron B. Champion, who was the organizer and newly installed president of the Red Stockings. Anxious to promote the commercial growth of Cincinnati, Champion viewed baseball as a vehicle for advertising the city and its products. In pursuit of his plan in 1868 he persuaded his directors to spend $11,000 to beautify the ball field and to equip the players. By standards of his day this was big money, but later that year Champion brashly promoted another $15,000 through the sale of new stock for the express purpose of buying the services of the best players in America. To insure top quality flesh for his money, Champion tried to lure the nine *New York Clipper* medal winners of 1868 to Cincinnati. In its modern application, such a plan might find a novice owner trying to buy up the members of the major league all-star team. To be charitable, such an idea, even in 1868, was unsophisticated. In those days players were unfettered by reserve clauses that tie today's men to single clubs, and thus they were free to go anywhere. But, in fact, most stars had strong personal attachments to their clubs, making the prospect of so many stars relocating in a town like Cincinnati rather unlikely.[10]

Nevertheless, then as now, stars liked to get more money, and the Cincinnati offer was a nice wedge for prying more money from their own clubs. Thus, it was not long before an unscrupulous pair pulled this trick: they first accepted the Cincinnati offer, then rejected it when more money was offered by their parent club. Naturally this treachery upset Champion, who already had publicized their acceptances and was now obliged to eat crow. After much blustering and a little fruitless legal maneuvering, Champion made his wisest decision. He entrusted scouting and recruiting to Manager Wright.

Certainly few men of the age knew more about the baseball talent market than Wright, who had the reputation of being "unapproachable in his good generalship and management."[11] Then, as later, Wright was guided by a belief that fans would pay to see well-trained and well-behaved players perform. Already he had tested the principle to his satisfaction, for in a single season he managed to transform the newly established Red Stocking club into the pride of Cincinnati. In a few weeks after receiving his new assignment, Wright completed the job of recruiting his 1869 dream team. As Wright saw it, only a few changes were necessary since the 1868 team already had six men good enough for the task. Besides himself, he retained catcher Douglas Allison, first baseman Charles Gould, dubbed "the bushel basket" for his sure hands, third baseman Fred Waterman, outfielder Calvin McVey, and the bearded pitching ace, Asa Brainard. In rounding out the 1869 team Wright snared outfielder Andy Leonard, second baseman Charles Sweasy, and utility man Dick Hurley from the ranks of his hometown rivals, the Cincinnati Buckeyes. Then for insurance Wright raided the Morrisania (N.Y.) Unions, picking up his brother George, a *Clipper* medalist, for shortstop, and Dave Birdsall for outfield duty. Thus, in efficient fashion Wright marshalled the

elite team that he proposed to lead on a nationwide tour, accepting challenges from any host that promised the Reds as
much as a third of the gate receipts.[12]

Normally the club existed on receipts, and the biggest capital expense was salaries. Contracts ran from March to
November, and some records show George Wright drawing
top pay at $1,400. Next came Harry at $1,200; Brainard
$1,100; Waterman $1,000; Sweasy, Gould, Allison, Leonard
and McVey $800 apiece; and Hurley $600. And even if
George Wright's later claim is correct, that Harry received
$2,000 and he $1,800, the fact remains that the first all-
salaried team was a modest investment.[13]

At the time investors thought the sum awesome and their
fears forced Wright to think in terms of big gate receipts,
toward which he directed his spartan training regimen. A
tireless drillmaster and clever teacher of tactics, he welded
the players into an efficient machine and won high praise
from Chadwick, who said that only when other managers
follow his lead, "may they expect a similar degree of
success."[14]

Along with his emphasis on training, Wright demonstrated
a flair for shrewd showmanship in his choice of team uniforms. In sending instructions to the club tailor, he ordered
bright red stockings to complement the white flannel shirts
and pants and the spiked Oxford shoes. This happy choice delighted local fans. Like the club's proud record of consecutive
victories, its colorful hose became its totem, and long after
Wright disbanded this team, other Cincinnati teams adopted
the red stockings as a trademark. Indeed, Cincinnati's current major league entry, nicknamed the Redlegs, after
McCarthy's red scare of the 1950s carried on the tradition.[15] In its own time the new style evoked criticism for
garishness, but in 1871 Chadwick credited the team for setting a new style trend toward "comfortably cool, tasteful"
baseball dress.[16]

Like Wright, the publicity-seeking Champion found his
niche as a club mythmaker. He arranged for a full-time re-

porter from the *Cincinnati Commercial* to cover the team and keep fans well supplied with fodder of the team's doings. Already in 1869 American baseball was a two-dimensional spectacle, one being the world of the playing field, and the other the world of baseball in the sporting pages. In 1869 Harry M. Millar got the job of covering the Reds, and he always licked the hand that fed him. His flow of copy, punctuated with admiration for Wright and high praise for the stars, helped build the legend of the immaculately conceived Reds—a spartan superteam molded by the ethic of hard work.

Millar accurately forecast a long winning streak when he described the team as "so well regulated that it should avail itself of its capabilities of defeating every club with which it contests." Millar's awkward forecast came on the eve of the club's departure for the East, where its reputation would be tested against the best teams in the land. Until then the Reds fattened on weaker rivals and local "picked nines" in fashioning a string of seven straight victories. Moving east, the team added ten more wins before invading metropolitan New York for its moment of truth. In mid-June, Wright's team came to town and Champion's promotional campaign was in high gear, stressing the audacious courage of the western Cinderella team daring to confront the eastern titans in their home yards. The test came on June 14 when, before a partisan crowd of 8,000 at Brooklyn's Union Grounds, the Reds downed the powerful Mutuals, 4–2. This was the victory Champion had dreamed of, and, when his announcement hit Cincinnati, joy reigned and streets filled with cheering fans. "Go on with your noble work," rang a congratulatory telegram. "Our expectations have been met." [17]

Unruffled by praise, Wright's team continued to defeat the eastern powers and to attract ever larger crowds. In Washington the players met President Grant, "who treated them cordially and complimented them on their play." Later at the game a writer commented that the Reds drew the "most aristocratic assemblage . . . that ever put in an appearance at a baseball match." [18]

As the Reds rode the crest of the victory wave, more sophisticated journals took note. *Harper's Weekly* published half a page of drawings of the "picked nine" and included a team picture showing grim, young faces fortified by beards and sideburns. But such praise was merely a warm-up for the homecoming reception that awaited in Cincinnati. Returning home late in June, the Reds found a joyous welcome and were drowned in local pride. The open hero worship lasted for days until the *Commercial* at last tried to dampen its excesses, complaining that some rabid fans of the moment hardly understood the game, citing one aged fan who admitted that he knew little "about baseball, or town ball, now-a-days, but it does me good to see those fellows. They've done something to add to the glory of our city." And a companion put a finger on the cause of their joy—"Glory, they've advertised the city—advertised us, sir, and helped our business, sir."

The glow lingered for weeks, but the great moment came the first day when Champion accepted a gift of a twenty-seven foot bat from a local lumber company on which were painted the names of all the heroes. All day long Champion and the team went from one fete to another, with the climax coming at a gala ball lasting until early morning. There, relaxing under the "Welcome Red Stockings" banner, the giddy Champion allowed that at the moment being president of the Reds was the highest office in America.[19]

After this fete came a long homestand with the Reds maintaining a winning pace, although once tied by the "Haymakers" of Troy, New York. The official account of this blotch on the team's escutcheon is a hurried blur, with Troy blamed for unsportsmanlike conduct. As the tale goes, in the fifth inning with the score tied at 17-all, the Troy captain picked a quarrel with the umpire. In a moment the argument grew hot and the captain, joined by the Troy club president, cursed the umpire and ordered the Haymakers off the field. This threatened to turn the crowd into a mob but the emotion was dissipated when the umpire forfeited the game to the

Reds. At the time the *Commercial* blamed the incident on New York gamblers, allegedly led by Congressman John Morrissey, the kingpin of the lot. As the *Commercial* explained, Morrissey stood to lose $17,000 if the Reds won, so he ordered the phoney incident. But others argued differently, and later the judiciary committee of the National Association disallowed the forfeit and ruled the contest a tie.[20]

Otherwise the Reds continued their winning ways and staged a triumphant march through the West, closing out their 1869 season with fifty-seven wins, a tie, and no defeats. In reading the official summary one is persuaded that the feat was entirely due to clean living, hard work, and shrewd capitalist acumen.

But if the record was Olympian, the men who achieved it were patently human. To read Harry Wright's diary account is to share the mixed joys and to understand some of his problems in managing this team of "supermen." Often the team drew well, like the time 15,000 saw them play in Philadelphia, or the 23,217 total for six games in New York which returned $4,474 in receipts. On the other hand there were days when the club might have stayed home. In Mansfield, Ohio, the Reds collected a mere $50, and in Cleveland, $81. And when the team arrived for a game in Syracuse, New York, Wright was horrified to find a live pigeon shoot taking place at the ball field, where the outfield grass was a foot high and the fence in a shambles. Upon inquiring, Wright learned that nobody remembered scheduling a ball game, so the Reds and their manager settled for the therapeutical consolation of a salt bath at a local spa at a cost of 35 cents.

Hard after this disappointment came another in Rochester. Arriving there Wright found the park in good shape with an eager crowd on hand. But with the game barely underway, a freak cloudburst soaked the field. Wright was equal to the challenge. Determined to save the receipts, he and his men "got some brooms, swept the water off, and put sawdust in the muddy places and commenced playing again."

Wright's diary also dispels the myth of his team's Sunday

school decorum. Although well-trained and disciplined, his boyish players kicked their heels. Often they straggled, missed trains, and ducked practices. The worst offender was pitcher Brainard, but even brother George cut practices. Brainard's odd personality led him into a variety of troubles. This made it tough for Wright, since the pitcher was a key man and the style of the time called for one pitcher to work nearly every game. This demand was less rigorous than it sounds since the pitching distance at the time was only forty-five feet and pitchers threw underhanded. But it was Wright's lot to be saddled with a good pitcher whose hypochondria always vaguely flared up. Brainard needed constant cajoling, and when the best arguments failed, Wright pitched himself, using a baffling "dewdrop" to hold down the enemy while his mates slugged away harder than usual.

If Brainard's miseries were not enough, he was also a night owl. Once when the exhausted team detrained in Buffalo at 4 A.M., everybody willingly took to bed except the pitcher and his pal, Fred Waterman, who chose to roam the streets looking for action. Yet withal Wright knew that Brainard was one of the best hurlers in the country, a man who battled like a demon in tough contests although he loafed sometimes when the going was easy. Because of Brainard's negligence, Wright frequently threatened him with fines. On top of all this, Brainard was flaky; in George Wright's words, he got "odd notions." Once during a game a wild rabbit scampered across the diamond passing in front of Brainard, who forgot batter and runners and threw at the bunny. The impulsive act cost the Reds two runs while the rabbit escaped untouched.[21]

Nor did Wright's troubles end with players' personality problems. A constant vigilance was needed to keep the spirited team off bottled spirits. Although Wright was a temperance man, he was wise enough to know that he lived in an age when the ability to hold hard liquor was a measure of one's manhood. That Wright fought a losing battle with John Barleycorn was apparent, when in 1870 the *Commercial* announced that the personal contracts of the Red Stockings terminated November 15, and "No player will be accepted next year who will not contract to abstain from intoxicating beverages at all times, unless prescribed by a physician in good standing." [22]

With enough internal problems to vex a missionary, Wright also faced the external problem of growing envy among the opposition. As victories mounted, the Reds became the target of mounting jealousy. Partisan newsmen whipped up emotions, and after the Reds' march through New York, Gotham papers sneered at the team's brand of professionalism. One editor argued that any player who works for pay ought to be "disgraced" or fired if he holds a commercial job since all professionals are security risks for bribes. It was argued that all such players were at the "beck and call of the sporting men, who bring them into the ring, game-cock fashion, and pit them against each other for money." [23]

Meanwhile other detractors disparaged the "eclectic" character of the Reds. This implied that a respectable team ought to use only native sons, a ridiculous charge that not only failed to consider the mobility of most Americans but also ignored the "eclectic" character of Wright's rivals. Yet Wright was powerless to fend off the attacks, and he consoled himself in the hope that it would take a year at least for rivals to catch up with his team in organization and training.

But Wright was wrong. After winning the first twenty-seven games in the 1870 campaign, his team faced another moment of truth on June 14. In Brooklyn, a likely place for the rise and fall of baseball dynasties, the avenging team was the Brooklyn Atlantics. Playing at the Capitoline Grounds, the Reds suffered their first defeat since late 1868 (after winning eighty-one, eighty-four, eighty-seven, or ninety-two straight, depending on how one counts informal games), by a score of 8–7. With the game tied 5–5 in regulation time, Wright might have settled for a draw, but with Champion's approval he chose to gamble on an extra inning victory. At the end of the tenth, the score remained tied. Then the Reds took the lead in the top of the eleventh, but Brooklyn pushed winning runs across in their half, aided by errors by second baseman Sweasy. Lacking none of the storied enthusiasm of Brooklyn sports crowds, this one went after the Reds with vengeance. One overeager fan jumped on the back of outfielder McVey as he attempted to field a ball, thus assisting one of the Brooklyn runners in scoring in the eleventh. After the victory a mob of fans made the Reds run a gauntlet of jeers and catcalls before the team made it to their carriage. With the team riding in an open carriage, their ordeal lasted all the way to the hotel where Champion in the safety of his room broke down and wept. Later he wired the *Commercial*: "Atlantics 8, Cincinnatis 7. The finest game ever played. Our boys did nobly, but fortune was against us. Eleven innings played. Though defeated, not disgraced."[24]

The wide publicity given this defeat testified to the rising tide of public interest in big-time baseball. For this interest the Reds can take only modest credit, for the boom was afoot before 1868 and continued after the Reds slipped from the top. Indeed, it is remarkable how quickly fans everywhere forgot the Reds in defeat. This was a lesson later generations of owners would know well, but it seemed harshly brutal to Champion. But falling attendance and another loss, this time at the hands of Chicago, raised a stockholder revolt that cost him his presidency. With a new regime committed to austerity, even though the books balanced, the Wright brothers knew that Cincinnati was no place for big-time baseball. Hard after Champion's ouster, the Wrights announced their decision to move to Boston where more money awaited both, and where Wright would build the Boston Red Stockings into the perennial champions of the first major league.

Behind him, in Cincinnati, he left a legend—the tale of the immaculate conception of major league baseball. That the play-for-pay movement in baseball has an older, evolutionary history is now well established, but the myth of the undefeated Reds as inspired innovators remains entrenched in official baseball sources and in the minds of fans.

NOTES

1. See Voigt, *American Baseball* (1966), pp. 3–13, for details.

2. *Philadelphia North American and United States Gazette,* June 10, 1864; and Fred Lieb, *The Baltimore Orioles* (New York: Rees Press, 1953), p. 6.

3. Harry Wright, Note and Account Books, Vol. I, Spalding Collection, New York Public Library; and Henry Chadwick, Scrapbooks, Vol. I, 17, Spalding Collection, New York Public Library.

4. Chadwick's column, *Sporting Life,* Jan. 26, 1887.

5. *Sporting News,* Dec. 14, 1895; and *Washington Star,* Aug. 14, 1927, Oct. 1, 1953.

6. Wright, Note and Account Books, I.

7. Chadwick, Scrapbooks, I, 17.

8. *Ibid.,* I, 17–18; see also *New York Clipper,* Feb. 13 and 20, 1869.

9. John Kiernan, "Harry Wright," article in Dumas Malone, ed., *Dictionary of American Biography* (New York, 1936), XX, 554. See also Allan Nevins, *The Emergence of Modern America,* 1865–1878 (New York: Macmillan, 1928), p. 217.

10. *New York Clipper,* April 30, 1969; *Sporting Life,* Jan. 23, 1884; Harry Ellard, *Baseball in Cincinnati: A History* (Cincinnati: Johnson and Hardin, 1907), pp. 138–209.

11. *New York Clipper,* Jan. 9, 1869; March 13, 1869; Chadwick, Scrapbooks, VI, 21.

12. *Cincinnati Commercial,* Aug. 26, Sept. 3, 1968; Ellard, *Baseball,* pp. 138–54.

13. *Ibid.,* 142; *St. Louis Globe Democrat,* Oct. 5, 1884.

14. Chadwick, Scrapbooks, VI, 21.

15. Ellard, *Baseball,* pp. 83–84.

16. *De Witt's Baseball Guide, 1871,* p. 94.

17. Ellard, *Baseball,* pp. 154–58; Chadwick, Scrapbooks, VI, 21–24.

18. Ellard, *Baseball,* pp. 161–62.

19. *Harper's Weekly,* July 3, 1869; July 2, 1870; *Cincinnati Commercial,* July 1, 2, 3, 1869.

20. *Cincinnati Commercial,* Aug. 27, 28; Sept. 1, 3, 6, 1869. Ellard, *Baseball,* pp. 166–69; Chadwick's *Baseball Manual, 1871,* p. 96.

21. Wright, Note and Account Books, I; Harry Wright, Correspondence of Harry Wright, V, 236–37, Spalding Collection, New York Public Library; Chadwick, Scrapbooks, I, 26; *Reach Official Baseball Guide, 1894,* pp. 79–85.

22. *Cincinnati Commercial.* Oct. 29, 1870.

23. Voigt, *Baseball* (1966), p. 32.

24. Ellard, *Baseball,* pp. 189, 190–95; Cincinnati *Commercial,* June 15, 1970.

3

Baseball's lost centennial*

"America's tragedy," as George Bernard Shaw once dubbed American baseball, celebrated the one-hundredth anniversary of its major league form in 1971, but few fans were aware of the fact. Ordinarily such an event would have baseball publicity mills working overtime grinding out epochal memorabilia. Instead they stood strangely idle, as if in a conspiracy of silence. Instead of 1871, official eyes focused on 1876, the year the National League was founded. This of course postpones the rites of intensification until 1976. Just why goes beyond antiquariana and into the realm of baseball mythology. Once answered it offers understanding of the web of relationships that binds ballplayers to their clubs.

A tempting answer to why the 1871 founding date was ignored would be that baseball publicists are simply ill versed in the game's nineteenth century history. This is certainly true for the era of 1871 to 1875 when the newborn National Association of Professional Base Ball Players furnished fans with their first major league thrills. Even the authoritative

*First published in *Journal of Popular Culture,* Vol. 5 (Summer 1971).

Macmillan *Encyclopedia* of the major league game ignores the era of the old National Association, despite available records in surviving guidebooks and accounts of its games in journals like the *New York Clipper*.

But faulting baseball publicists for being lightweight historians only beclouds a more basic explanation for passing up a gala celebration in 1971. More likely the real reason is embedded in the very title of America's first major baseball league—the National Association of Professional Base Ball *Players*. It was a league of professional players, organized by players who enjoyed complete freedom of contract and mobility. True, clubowners financed the teams, but most of these investors were gentlemen sportsmen who as stockholders willingly passed up profits in hopes of buying public esteem by their conspicuous consumption.

In brief an artist-patron pattern characterized the relationships between owners and players in the early 1870s. For their part, owners derived satisfaction from beating rival owners in the baseball matches. And the intense rivalry generated by their will to win prompted owners to employ good players as early as 1860.

By 1870 the multitude of paid players so alarmed officials of the National Association of Amateur Base Ball Players that they decided to call a halt. At a stormy meeting late in 1870 amateur interests and mercenary interests clashed violently, forcing the mercenaries to walk out. Since at the time the amateurs controlled the organized game, their policy was to wait for the professionals to submit to terms.

Belatedly a group of professional players decided to defy the amateurs by picking up the gauntlet and moving to organize a new league. For this purpose they met on a rainy St. Patrick's night in 1871 at the Colliers Rooms in New York City. With little drama they created the first professional major league in a few hours, using the simple device of rewriting the old amateur constitution with the word "professional" inserted in the right spots. They requested and used a copy of the playing rules from the amateur organization.

Shortly thereafter the first major league opened play with clubs organized on an East-West basis. Western strongholds included Chicago, Rockford (Ill.), Fort Wayne, and Cleveland arrayed against teams from eastern sites such as New York, Troy, Philadelphia, Washington, and Boston.

It was all surprisingly easy since the professionals found their amateur rivals to be paper tigers. The amateurs mounted no counterattack; they even failed to field a league, and the old organization faded away, "dying of inanition, after an inane and inocuous existence."

With the field to themselves, America's first major league began a five-year history in 1871. Although it proved to be a jerry-built structure that wheezed along with more problems than triumphs, the league's solid achievements were portentous. Above all, it was a players' league and it quickly established the professional baseball player as an American culture hero. With this status went publicity and with publicity came higher salaries. At least one player knocked down a $4,500 annual salary and Boston's 1875 team payroll topped $30,000, a figure unmatched by any of the National League successor teams until the early 1880s.

For fans, the National Association proved to be an attractive spectacle, offering five years of good play. In this time the Association established the precedent of instigating and charting the basic changes in the game of baseball. Thereafter all basic changes in baseball were handed down from the major leagues. Moreover, individual managers like Harry Wright, whose Boston Red Stockings won four straight pennants after losing the 1871 race to Philadelphia, developed basic techniques for coping with ticket sales, public accommodations, groundskeeping, and other problems of club management on the one hand, while working out systems for paying, training, directing, and disciplining players on the other. Wright in 1874 even found time to take his champion Reds to England in a missionary campaign aimed at spreading baseball to the motherland. It bombed because the cricket clubs which hosted the games did not like what they saw.

But an ocean of problems swamped these successes. One of the worst problems was the haphazard scheduling system that required club secretaries to write opponents and negotiate playing dates. Equally uncertain was the umpiring, which was casually chosen and unpaid. Nor was anything done to curb the movements of bribe-minded gamblers at the parks. Indeed, an excess of freedom killed America's first major league. Entry into the league was so free that any club might join by simply forwarding an application accompanied by a $10 entry fee. Compare this free approach to landing a major league franchise with the millions extracted for such a privilege today! But the results of the Association's open policy were predictable—many lightweight clubs tried the major league route, but after absorbing a few lumps they dropped out, to the bewilderment of fans and the frustration of those leaders who preferred an orderly league.

Naturally in such a free atmosphere players who controlled the league exercised full freedom. Contracts were renegotiated annually since no reserve clause bound a player to a club. Not surprisingly many jumped, or "revolved" as the practice was called in the 1870s.

Had there been a dozen managers as serious and as enterprising as Harry Wright, who was able to attract, to train, and to discipline promising players into a winning team, the Association might still be in business. But there was only one Wright, and when his team dominated the Association as major league baseball's first awesome dynasty, winning four pennants, the last in 1875 on an incredible 71–8 record, his very success undermined the league. The end came in 1876 when money-minded promoters, with the help of men like Wright, replaced the players' league with the National League of Professional Base Ball *Clubs*. Once again the title told the tale, for players now found themselves bound to club interests by such devices as the reserve clause and blacklistings.[1]

From time to time ballplayers fought to regain the basic rights that were theirs under the first major league. Once, in 1890, they established their own league, but usually they gained power only when some interloping major league challenged the established supremacy of the National League of Professional Base Ball *Clubs*. Usually such player revolts were brief, nasty, and abortive. When productive of some success, as when the American League successfully challenged the National League in 1901, the leaders of the interloping league joined forces with the National in a "National Agreement" merger of interests that included the ever controversial reserve clause.

Today's ballplayers are better equipped to fight back, as indicated by Curt Flood's abortive suit, Catfish Hunter's successful suit, Congressional investigations, and the activities of the Players' Association under Marvin Miller's guidance. Moreover, outside of baseball, players in the professional basketball leagues have an excellent grasp of the principle involved, as evidenced by their antitrust action to forestall a merger of the National Basketball Association with the American Basketball Association.

In the light of these present controversies it is not surprising that major league baseball owners and officials would not want to be reminded of a time when major league baseball belonged to the players. Although the history of the 1871 major league showed the serious limitations to profiteering under a player controlled system, no owner can claim that today's player demands for decision making rights or power are "unprecedented." Because they established America's first major league, players of today are missing a telling propaganda blow by submitting to the official celebration of 1976 as the centennial of the major league game.

NOTES

1. Voigt, *American Baseball* (1966), chap. 4.

4

The Boston Red Stockings: The birth of major league baseball*

In recent years baseball fans have endured round after round of commemorative anniversaries from the baseball publicity mills. From the 1969 centennial of the Cincinnati Reds as inventors of the professional game,[1] to the impending 1976 centennial of the National League as America's first major league, such displays have an epochal quality. Celebrated in literature, films, and oratory—often with questionable historical accuracy—they function as rites of intensification for restoring baseball's legitimacy, longevity, and virility. To the historian of sport with a trained suspicion of myth, such celebrations are a challenge to set the record straight. Even if it means foisting still another celebration upon baseball fans, let it be said that 1971 was the true centennial of major league baseball.

In 1871 the first major league was launched and its brief five-year history was a glorious era for New England fans. Operating under the unwieldy title of the National Association of Professional Base Ball Players, the league was a

---

*First published in the *New England Quarterly*, Vol. 43, No. 4 (Dec. 1970), 531–49.

shoddy structure that muddled through five campaigns before succumbing to the National League coup of 1876. But
while it lasted the Association was Boston's pride. That
Boston ever had an entire age of baseball glory may surprise
present-day Red Sox fans, some of whom are old enough to
recall the grim days of much promise and little success (or
the even grimmer days of the National League Braves, Bees,
Rustlers, Doves, and Beaneaters, as Boston's entry was variously dubbed).

At the birth of major league baseball in 1871, Boston's
mighty presence was felt from the start. Boston manager
William Henry (Harry) Wright helped to organize the league
and then guided the Boston Red Stockings to four consecutive pennants, narrowly missing a clean sweep of five in a
row. Moreover, his stars now occupy niches in Baseball's Hall
of Fame at Cooperstown, and his standards, laid down as
manager and innovator, remain part of baseball's operating
machinery.

The American baseball scene of 1871 was a propitious time
for staging the coup that would bring on the first major
league. Public enthusiasm was booming even more than it did
in the late 1850s. And if the Civil War temporarily checked
the spread of the game, that conflict helped to bring baseball
to regions where it was previously unknown. With peace restored, the game's popularity reached a new high. Clubs were
learning that fans would pay to watch the games, but good
players were learning that they could command high pay for
their services. Since most teams were paying players by 1869,
the decision of the Cincinnati Reds to field an all-professional
team only hastened a trend already afoot. Managed by
"Harry" Wright, the Reds compiled a long skein of victories
into the middle of 1870. By the end of that year, enough
other teams were following the Reds' example so as to foment
a crisis in the promotion of baseball.

Until 1871 organized baseball was loosely headed by the
National Association of Base Ball Players, a league committed
to amateur principles. Under its slack rules most clubs were

run by gentlemen sportsmen whose motives were partly prompted by the snobbery of conspicuous leisure. But in their competing with one another, winning became a dominant motive, prompting a competitive search for the best available talent. Although the practice was condemned by Association leaders, the purists were forced to give grudging recognition to the persistent professionals, who played for "money, place, or emolument." Once legitimized the trend continued until the fearful amateurs determined to stamp out professionalism. In the fall of 1870 at the annual Association meeting, the amateurs withdrew after a hot verbal battle. Being in the majority, they thought they could force the professionals to come to terms, perhaps to a compromise that would heal the breach and make possible an orderly campaign in 1871. By maintaining control over the legitimate league in American baseball, the amateurs counted on the professionals' begging to be let in from the cold.

The gauntlet thus flung remained on the ground for some time. Meanwhile, the professionals agonized over the question of whether to fight or to surrender. From their vantage point it was a tough decision, and each passing month made submission seem more likely. By March 1871, there was still no decision. Since the baseball season customarily ran from late March to November, there was little time to spare. Their power lay in the expanding professional movement, with western centers like Chicago, Cleveland, Rockford, and Fort Wayne joining with eastern bastions in Boston, Washington, Philadelphia, New York, and Troy. It was enough to fashion a new league. At this eleventh hour, the professionals decided upon a bold stroke.

On a windy, rainy St. Patrick's night the professional delegates journeyed to the Colliers Rooms, a high-class saloon in New York City. Aware of a pressing need for action and their responsibilities to the hundred paid players whom they represented, the delegates were duty bound to act. Brushing aside animosities, the delegates set about the business at hand. All knew that only one evening could be spared for the task of building a league. As a guide they had only the loose constitution of the National Association, but this document became their model.

In an unusual atmosphere of "good feeling," leaders were quickly selected: James Kearns of the Athletics served as chairman; Norman "Nick" Young of Washington was secretary; and "Harry" Wright, recently hired to manage the Boston Club, headed the steering committee. Thus organized, the delegates moved to name the new league the National Association of Professional Base Ball Players. This conservative decision showed a reluctance to depart from the familiar organization pattern. Yet by today's standards it was a radical move, since the term "professional players" underscored the league's commitment to player interests.

In drafting a constitution, the delegates moved quickly. A *New York Clipper* reporter was impressed: "The moment the association had been permanently organized everything went on as harmoniously as a club meeting. In fact, we have never attended any convention of the fraternity which reflected so much credit on the delegates and the clubs they so ably represented."

Anxious to entice any support, the rebels kept the structure of the new league loose and flexible. To gain entrance, all a club needed to do was to petition the steering committee and enclose a $10 entry fee. Today millions are paid for a major league franchise, but in 1871 the delegates apologized for charging $10, explaining that it was necessary to purchase the annual pennants!

But the very openness of the new league hurt when it came to the matter of scheduling games. Instead of a fixed schedule, each club merely agreed to meet a rival five times with dates to be arranged between the two contenders. The championship was to go to the team with the most victories. In the event of a tie, the steering committee was empowered to decide which team had the better claim. The only strict rule called on each team to finish play by the first of November because the pennant presentation was set for November 15.

At this point the meeting fell into disorder as delegates milled around trying to schedule choice rivals on the most advantageous playing dates. Rockford, Cleveland, and Chicago quickly set up a three-week eastern tour, and the Washington Olympics planned a fortnight's northern trip. But the schedule was a thing of shreds and patches. So casual were agreements that managers spent hours jockeying for dates. But this was the way of baseball's "gentlemen's era." In retaining the same lax structure as did the old amateur association, the first major league shortened its own life. Not until the National League was born was the remedy of a fixed schedule adopted and successfully enforced.

In other ways these conservative radicals clung to time-worn customs. For instance, they managed to save time and energy by adopting the constitution of the old amateur association. The rebels might have avoided future trouble by creating a professional staff of umpires, but they continued to rely on unpaid volunteers, usually affiliated with the club and often deficient in experience. The sole requirement was that an umpire be "acknowledged as competent." The home team was given the advantage of selecting an umpire, but if he failed to appear at game time, the rival captains were to agree on a substitute. This incredibly casual approach to a vital part of the game caused the infant major league endless embarrassments.

Another weakness cropped up when the delegates failed to agree on a uniform ticket price. Most favored a 50 cents unit price with two-thirds of the proceeds for the home team and the balance for the visitors. When the matter went unresolved, the omission proved crippling. In defense of the half-dollar rate, Wright fought some of his most stubborn battles with rival managers. This unsettled issue plagued major league baseball throughout the nineteenth century.

But at this point in major league history, indecision was the price of harmony. Cooperation was necessary to get the league going, but the planners soon discovered the high costs of laxity. Another stumbling block came from inability to protect the game from gamblers. When the National League plotters overthrew the Association in 1876, one of their most damaging attacks was the corruption issue.

But such dangers lay in the distant future. At this point the Association planners considered their job to be done. After instructing Secretary Young to write the old amateur association for copies of its playing rules, the delegates enjoyed their refreshments and disbanded.[2]

In retrospect the results were conservative rather than revolutionary. But despite the unwieldy and unrealistic legislating, it was a memorable evening's work. A commercial major league was born that would have far-reaching impact upon such diverse groups as players, owners, stockholders, sportswriters, and spectators. Had the delegates shaped a permanent institution in a single evening, using no guide but the shopworn amateur constitution, it would have been a miracle. Although it was not a night of miracles the creation did provide fans with the delights of five years of first-rate baseball.

Happily for the planners their revolt went unchallenged. The old amateur association never recovered; a half-hearted effort in 1872 to organize amateurs into a new association failed in 1874. Thus by default the professionals gained control of organized baseball. From 1871 onward, changes in rules and style of play were dictated by professionals. Much later, groups like the National Amateur Athletic Union, the college associations, and softball leagues gained some influence, but the main course of baseball evolution was charted by organized professionals.[3]

With their new league afloat, the professionals anticipated a wide-open race for cash and glory. Within weeks nine clubs entered the lists, all from eastern and midwestern sections of the land. With the South reeling from the effects of war, and the Far West too remote for the transportation services of the day, the association's boast of being a national organization was dubious. But hopes ran high. Chicago, heading a western division which included teams from Rockford, Fort Wayne, and Cleveland, proudly opened its new Lake Front Park, capable of seating 7,000 shaded spectators, with a special sec-

tion for ladies and dignitaries. With money flowing freely, the
Chicago White Stockings boasted that one player would receive $4,500 for his services.[4]

But most sportswriters were impressed by the potential of
such eastern clubs as the New York Mutuals and Philadelphia Athletics. Of doubtful promise were such contenders as
Troy, Washington, and Boston. But Wright's presence with
Boston soon revised these early forecasts.

Midway in the 1870 season, soon after his Cincinnati Reds
ended their record victory skein, Wright announced his inten-
tion of moving to Boston. The announcement was a stunning
coup for President Ivers Adams, who headed the newly
formed Boston club. With the news went word that Wright's
brother George, the peerless shortstop, was to be part of the
package. For his services as player-manager, Wright was to
get $2,500, considerably more than Cincinnati would pay. In-
deed, so disheartened were the Cincinnati directors over the
Reds' failure to make money that they voted to drop their
professional experiment. This freed the Wrights to seek
greener pastures and to entice such stars as McVey, Leonard,
Birdsall, and Gould to come with them.[5]

With such proven stars as a nucleus, Wright swiftly employed his vast knowledge of the talent market to recruit a
formidable team for Boston. Boldly expropriating the proud
label, "Red Stockings," for his team, Wright drew angry protests from Cincinnatians, but his team soon demonstrated
their ability to live up to the name. As pitcher, Wright selected Albert Goodwill Spalding, the nineteen-year-old prod-
igy of the Rockford team. Already acclaimed as one of the
best pitchers in the land, the ambitious Spalding had pin-
point control and his jerky, underhand delivery was most
deceptive. Writers also wrote glowingly of his speed. One said
it had "the precision and rapidity of a cannon shot." At six
feet, one inch, Spalding was one of the tallest men in the
league and his ambitions exceeded his height. Shrewd, calcu-
lating, a born promoter, he viewed baseball as a stepping-
stone to a profitable career in industry. When he felt the time
to be ripe for such a move, he would abandon Boston for

Chicago. From there he went on to launch a career in the promising sporting goods industry while remaining a power in major league councils until his death in 1915. Such attainments, however, lay in the future; from 1871 to 1875 he was Wright's pitching staff in an age when a club depended on a single strong arm.[6]

The other stars on Wright's team included his brother George, a fine fielding and hitting shortstop, and little Roscoe (Ross) Barnes, the second baseman. Signed as a rookie in 1871, Barnes took advantage of a rule permitting "fair-foul" hitting to become the Association's perennial batting champ. Such hits had only to touch fair territory before rolling foul, and Barnes became the master of this technique of hitting. So long as the Association lasted, this rule was in, but when the National League abolished the rule, Barnes' sun set rapidly.

With another rookie, Harry Schafer, installed at third, Wright had a first-class team. That year the Red Stockings battled the Philadelphia Athletics and Chicago White Stockings to the last day. The three-way race made the 1871 campaign memorable, with disaster and discord heightening the dramatic impact. Disaster struck Chicago's team when the terrible fire destroyed the club's physical assets, forcing the players to play all remaining games on the road. The White Stockings fought heroically, aided by free railroad tickets, and generous offers of hospitality from rivals. Until the last day they remained in the race, but lost to the Athletics in a poorly attended game. Their motley appearance saddened a reporter who wrote: "Not one of the nine were dressed alike, all the uniforms having been consumed at the fire. They presented a most extraordinary appearance from the particolored nature of their dress. All who could get white stockings did so, but they were not many."[7]

In the wake of the Chicago tragedy, discord upset the infant league in the angry rivalry between the Athletics and Wright's Reds. Overcoming racking injuries that hampered the team's midseason efforts, Boston came on strong in the stretch, finishing with twenty-two wins and ten losses. Since the Athletics posted a 22–7 record, the championship committee awarded the pennant to Philadelphia. But Wright charged the committee with dishonest favoritism, challenging some Athletic victories scored against teams with ineligibles in their lineups. Wright also argued that league rules required each team to play a total of forty games. Although none did, the Boston record of thirty-two complete games came closest to the mark, and since the team having the most victories was to win, Wright argued that his team deserved the honor.[8] Obviously the Association was suffering from its hasty job of organizing, and when one discouraged club fell by the wayside, to be replaced by a substitute which had to inherit the collapsed club's won and loss record, the confusion was confounded.

When Wright's protest was disallowed, the Athletics in a front-page woodcut in the *Clipper* were touted as champions of the United States. As pictured, they were a fierce-looking crew. All wore blazers and sported mustaches, except for pitcher Dick McBride, whose fierce sideburns compensated for a naked upper lip. And America's first major league champions contained some famous stars. The battery included McBride and catcher Fergus Malone. The infield had Wes Fisler at first, Al Reach at second, Levi Meyerle at third, and John Radcliff at short. In the outfield the regulars were John Sensenderfer, George Heubel, and Ed Cuthbert. Hicks Hayhurst managed the youthful team, who averaged twenty-five years of age. Financially the team did well, returning $200 in dividends to the stockholders after salaries and expenses totaling $22,457.14 were paid.[9] In the gentleman's era of American baseball, where prestige counted more than profit to stockholders, this was a successful season.

For America's new breed of professional baseball players, 1871 was a good year. When winter cooled the ragings of the previous season, the annual meeting of the Association strengthened players' control by the election of Robert Ferguson as president. Henceforth, it was resolved that only a player might serve as president of the league. This important but short-lived policy meant that the Association was to be a worker's paradise.[10] That player control over major league baseball failed to survive the Association era owed to a lack of business and administrative acumen among players. Such skill, however, did repose among club directors, whose ranks grew to include a profit-minded minority eager to promote baseball as a profitable business. Once in power after encouraging the National League coup, they promptly substituted the ethic of business enterprise for that of player welfare.

But for the moment at least players called the tune, although forces were working to end their dominance. The excessive freedom of players was not the only factor undermining the Association. The season of 1871 exposed a problem of shaky franchises as Fort Wayne withdrew and was replaced by the Brooklyn Eckfords. When this warning passed unheeded, and nothing was done to tighten entrance requirements, other weak franchises in subsequent seasons chose the dropout route.

Ironically, the growing Boston power increased the Association's dropout problem. Bent on avenging his narrow 1871 defeat, Wright grimly prepared for 1872. Besides his own perfectionist standards, Wright now had a personal score to settle with Athletic manager, Hayhurst. Just after winning the 1871 pennant, Hayhurst penned a sarcastic letter to Wright asking his advice on where to display the pennants. Wright replied caustically: "I think the proper place is or would be the Athletic club room, or some place where *all* who wish could go and see them." After all, Wright chided, the Athletics are "the first legal and recognized champions of the United States," and they ought to "elevate the National game." [11]

The season of 1872 renewed the bitter feud. That nine other clubs also nursed pennant hopes mattered little to these protagonists; five teams were so outclassed that they dropped out early. In the Philadelphia-Boston rivalry, the Athletics drew first blood, beating Boston in Philadelphia early in the season. But the Red Stockings, bolstered by the presence of a new first baseman, Fraley Rogers, who teamed with Barnes, George Wright, and Schafer in the infield, reeled off nineteen straight victories. Then when the Athletics came to town for a rematch, it seemed to an awed reporter that "all Boston took a half holiday." The fans' blood thirst was satiated when the Reds crushed the Athletics, 13–4. A highlight was a fine running catch by Harry Wright: "As the veteran came in from the field cheer on cheer was given, which he very politely recognized by lifting his hat." [12]

Fired by that victory, nothing stopped the Reds, who finished with thirty-nine wins and only eight losses. The Athletics were seven games behind, and for failing to live up to schedule commitments, their record was judged inferior to that of Baltimore and the New York Mutuals. As for the rest of the pack, only two finished the season. Among five dropouts, Washington's Nationals played and lost eleven games before quitting. Altogether the six weak sisters of the Association won only sixteen of ninety-four games played. [13]

Although victory heightened Boston's pride, the season of 1872 was profitless. Even Boston lost money, but the grateful club directors voted a new stock issue, enabling Wright to strengthen the team by adding rookies "Deacon" Jim White, a catcher, and Jim O'Rourke, a player versatile enough to play anywhere. Both were destined for long and brilliant major league careers. It was a wise move, sorely needed in 1873 when George Wright's rheumatism and other injuries crippled the team. By August the Reds lagged ten games behind the leader, a new Philadelphia franchise called the "Phillies" or "Whites." Overcoming such a lead looked hopeless, but a month of pressing brought Boston within two and a half games of first place. In September the Phillies faltered, losing five in a row, including one to Boston before a partisan Philadelphia crowd of 5,000. Riding their momentum, the Reds went on to post a 43–16 record, good enough to beat the Phillies, who were trailed by Baltimore, the Mutuals, the Athletics, and the Brooklyn Atlantics. As for the eight remaining hopefuls, only one dropped out, a record of sorts for the Association.[14]

The season of 1873 also was a financial bust, with only the players prospering. Although much blame was attributed to the business depression, officials of the Association decided that fans wanted a change in the game. At the annual meeting, it was decided to try a ten-man version of baseball. As suggested by Henry Chadwick, the sportswriter, the scheme called for a "right shortstop" to be posted between first and second base. Not only would it lend symmetry to the game, Chadwick argued, but it would free the first and third basemen to range into foul territory to chase elusive fair-foul hits. Although abandoned after a few games, the plan typifies the experimental temperment of baseball men, whose present-day schemes for improving the game have the precedent of a long tradition.[15]

By 1874 the pattern of Wright's ruthless domination of the Association was complete. With rookies White and O'Rourke blooded in the 1873 campaign, the team was set. As manager, the thirty-nine-year-old Wright could afford to sit out most games, trusting outfielding to Leonard, McVey, and George Hall, the latter recently acquired from Baltimore. The infield needed no help, and the battery of Spalding and White was the Association's finest. Wright now felt free to promote a cherished missionary venture—that of taking the team to his native England to promote baseball there. The expedition of 1874 required tight scheduling, but Wright handled the problem efficiently. Using Spalding as his emissary, and the Athletics as playing partners in the venture, the teams spent a month in England, the Reds taking eight of the fourteen games played against the Athletics. But the games drew poorly and baseball excited little interest. Worse, the American players returned home disenchanted over pay cuts forced on them because of the financial losses suffered abroad.[16]

Back in the States, the chastened missionaries of American baseball faced the task of finishing their 1874 campaign. To their earlier total of twenty wins, they added thirty-two more, enough for a 52–18 seasonal record which was good enough to defeat their closest rivals, the New York Mutuals, by seven-and-a-half games.[17]

Notwithstanding the unprecedented entry of thirteen teams in the 1875 race, or the fact that only a single team dropped out in 1874, the Association was sick unto death. At the close of 1874, contenders openly expressed a sense of futility in the face of Boston's domination. In that year, only Boston completed a full schedule. Ugly rumors of game selling also tarnished the Association's image. And outside Boston, defeat, debt, and mismanagement dulled the competitive spirit of the contestants. Nevertheless, the dawn of a new spring and the addition of five new entrants, including a third from Philadelphia, raised the hopes of contenders. Perhaps the time of release from Boston tyranny was at hand.

But the 1875 Boston Reds now stood at the pinnacle of their power. Spalding and Wright were an indomitable battery; McVey, Leonard, Beals, and Manning provided a hard-hitting outfield; the infield of O'Rourke, Barnes, George Wright, and Schafer was unequalled. With such power waiting to be unleashed, Wright fretted at the tardy arrival of spring. But when it came, Boston rolled up the league. Except for Chicago and the Athletics, who fought hard, the other entries were hopelessly outclassed. As the defeated ten daily counted dwindling gate receipts, some openly urged the breakup of Wright's Reds.

For a time Chicago hung in, but two crushing defeats by scores of 24–7 and 11–4 ended their hopes. Meanwhile the Athletics carried their rivalry to the league council rooms, where old feuds were rekindled. On the ball field, bitterness marked each Athletic-Boston clash. But nothing stopped the 1875 Boston charge. Of the Association's twenty leading hitters, eight, including the top four, were Boston men. The Reds won handily, posting an awesome 71–8 record, fifteen games up on its nearest pursuer. For the weaker half of the league, 1875 was a nightmare. Among the newcomers, only St. Louis finished, while six others left records of futility.

Keokuk won one of thirteen and quit; the Atlantics took two of forty-two and folded: and four others, with a combined record of seventeen wins and eighty-eight losses, dropped out.

On paper the key to Boston's superiority appeared to be the batting performances. But besides having the league's finest battery, records showed six Boston men topping all rivals in fielding their positions. Among these, George Wright posted his fifth consecutive season, leading the nation's shortstops. It is a tribute to Wright's players that in a gloveless age their fielding records approached modern standards.[18]

Peering behind the records, some of Wright's rivals thought that Boston's deadliest weapon was Wright himself, and they dubbed the Association, "Harry Wright's League." Certainly Wright was a baseball genius, who not only mastered the techniques of the game but possessed that vital "something extra" of which geniuses are made. Wright worked tirelessly on fundamentals. As he told a young rookie: "Learn to be a sure catch, a good thrower—strong and accurate—a reliable batter and a good runner, all to be brought out—if in you—by steady and persevering practice." [19] Disciplined practice was the *leitmotiv* of Wright's style. His men were masters of that disciplined efficiency now called teamwork. More than likely, Wright's cricket background influenced his tactics. He constantly experimented with drills to make his men work better together. By the 1880s his policy of pregame batting and fielding drills was widely imitated until today it is a standard procedure. While each of his men took a turn hitting, a fungo batter would stand farther down the line driving fly balls at outfielders.[20] Widely praised as superior to the old lackluster rite of warming up by balltossing, Wright's plan was called "scientific." Although his proposal to schedule a postseason play-off among the top teams proved profitless, it planted the germ of the modern World Series idea.[21]

But Wright was more than a drillmaster. As a tactician, he developed fielding strategies, including back-up plays for infielders and outfielders. That his system worked was evidenced by his ability to transform raw rookies into recognized stars.

His own self-image was that of a persistent teacher. He was irked when envious rivals sneered that anybody could win with Wright's team. Wright replied that managing a team involved skill in human relations and demanded that a manager regard a player as a bundle of promises and problems; even a star required "special handling." Wright repeatedly proved his expertise. In 1876 he made a star out of Tom Bond, a promising pitcher whose growth was stunted under another manager's harsh discipline.[22]

Wright's teams were models of efficiency, which reflected their manager's conviction that fans would pay to see well-coached teams. As for the players, Wright saw them as motivated by rational self-interest; they could expect high salaries only if they went beyond the line of duty. Wright's 1875 payroll of $20,000 was major league baseball's highest until the early 1880s.[23] While Wright's excess of faith in a rational approach sounds naive, Wright drove this ethic deeply into the rooting traditions of major league baseball promotion. Today vestiges of Wright's horsehide version of the Protestant Ethic survive, reminding modern players, owners, and managers of the game's gentlemanly heritage. It stands as a subtle barrier against those owners who would indulge in crass commercialism or hucksterism.

Measured by the standards of pennants and profits, no Association team matched Boston's success. With Wright handling administrative details, including scheduling, groundskeeping, ballpark supervision, while at the same time playing his position and riding herd on his men at home and on the road, he laid down standards of major league club administration. By 1875 he directed the spending of a $35,000 annual budget—a modest sum by today's standards, yet large enough to pioneer the uncharted world of baseball promotion. As a pioneer, he wrestled with ever persistent problems of administration including advertising, procurement, groundskeeping, travel scheduling, and salary negotiating.[24]

Had there been twelve men like Wright returning modest

profits to leisurely investors who in turn usually plowed profits back into the team, the Association might have survived. But elsewhere management was weak and investors chafed at losses, while the more mercenary elements dreamed of a major league controlled by owners in the interests of profiteering. Because the Association favored player interests, even Wright thought that salaries were too high, discipline overly lax, and player mobility appallingly disrupting.[25]

Bound as players were only by annual contracts, no manager knew when a star might be seduced away by a higher offer. Although Wright paid his men well, in 1875 a quartet of his superstars—the "big four" of Spalding, Barnes, White, and McVey—served notice that they would join the White Stockings in Chicago in 1876.[26] When Boston fans heard the news, they roasted the quartet, berating them as quitters and "seceders" at subsequent home games.

Meanwhile one of these secessionists, Spalding, was busily plotting to end the Association as a players' league and planning to replace it with a league of *clubs*, to be called the National League. Moreover, Spalding's scheme had Wright's blessing. "Professional clubs," Wright wrote to William Hulbert, the mastermind behind the National League coup, "to keep in existence, must have gate money, to receive gate money they must play games, and to enable them to play games, their opponents must have faith that such games will prove remunerative."

Backed by men like Harry Wright, the National League coup destroyed the Association as easily as the Association crushed the amateurs. After a few years, major league baseball proved profitable under the National League, and, with its reserve clause binding a player to a club, stability was achieved at the cost of player freedom. Further stability came by use of the device of screening franchise applicants, forcing them also to back their entry with earnest money. Thus was eliminated the pesky problem of clubs dropping out in midseason. But the success of the National League owed much to the pioneering of America's first major league, the National Association of Professional Base Ball Players.

As the Association's innovator *par excellence,* Wright deserves much credit. Yet Wright modestly, and with gentle humor, brushed aside Hulbert's suggestion that he would become "the father of the game." Having just watched his "seventh . . . base bawler" enter the world, Wright thought it burden enough "to be considered the father of this little game, but I wish it to go no further. Seven is plenty, thank you."[27] Such drollery marked the modesty of major league baseball's great innovator, but posterity owes him the honor of fully crediting him with laying the ground plan for a century of major league baseball.

NOTES

1. David Quentin Voigt, "America's First Red Scare—The Cincinnati Reds of 1869," *Ohio History,* Winter 1969.

2. *Proceedings of the National Association of Professional Baseball Players,* pp. 1–11; *New York Clipper,* March 25, 1871; and Voigt, *American Baseball* (1966), chap. 4.

3. Francis C. Richter, *Richter's History and Records of Baseball: The American Nation's Chief Sport* (Philadelphia: Sporting Life, 1914), pp. 39–40.

4. Voigt, *American Baseball,* (1966) pp. 34–38.

5. Voigt, "America's First Red Scare," p. 24.

6. *Rockford Register,* March 25, 1871; *Beadle Dime Baseball Player, 1872,* pp. 41–44.

7. *New York Clipper,* Oct. 14, 1871; Oct. 21, 1871; *Chicago Tribune,* Nov. 3, 1871.

8. *Chicago Tribune,* Nov. 10, 1871; Nov. 13, 1871; Nov. 26, 1871; *De Witt's Baseball Guide, 1872,* pp. 69, 90–91, and *1873,* p. 68.

9. *New York Clipper,* Nov. 18, 1871; *Philadelphia North American and United States Gazette,* Nov. 14, 1871.

10. Richter, *History and Records,* p. 44; *Beadle's 1872,* pp. 45–47.

11. Wright to E. Hicks Hayhurst. Correspondence of Harry Wright, V, 143–44.

12. Chadwick, Scrapbooks, I, 88.

13. *De Witt's Baseball Guide, 1873,* pp. 54–57, 68–69. Wright to Alex V. Davidson, Chairman of the Championship Committee, Oct. 30, 1872, Wright Correspondence, V. 464–66.

14. *Beadle's 1874,* pp. 49–50.

15. *Ibid.,* pp. 45–48; *1875,* pp. 45–46; *1876,* pp. 70–71; Richter, *History and Records,* pp. 39–49.

16. Albert G. Spalding, *America's National Game* (New York: American Sports, 1911), pp. 75–86. Adrian C. Anson, *A Ballplayer's Career* (Chicago: Era, 1900), pp. 75–85; *Beadle's 1875,* pp. 56–59.

17. Richter, *History and Records,* pp. 42–46.

18. *Beadle's 1876,* pp. 63–64. Alfred H. Spink, *The National Game: A History of Baseball* (St. Louis; Sporting News, 1910), pp. 90, 118, 220, 237, 257, 270.

19. Wright to Charles Tubbs, Dec. 2, 1874, Wright Correspondence, VI, 83–84.

20. Henry Chadwick, *The Art of Baseball Batting* (New York: A. G. Spalding, 1885), pp. 38–39; *New York Clipper,* Sept. 17, 1887.

21. Wright to James Moorhouse, May 15, 1873; Wright to F. Todd, April 18, 1875, Wright Correspondence, V;. *Boston Herald,* July 9, 1872.

22. Wright to Henry Chadwick, Jan. 2, 1875, Sept. 14, 1876, Wright Correspondence, VI.

23. *Beadle's 1876,* p. 67. A sample Boston contract is in Wright Correspondence, I.

24. *Beadle's 1876,* pp. 63–64. Wright to A. Childs, April 10, 1875; Wright to John Ryan, March 4, 1872. Wright Correspondence, V, VI. Wright, Note and Account Books, II.

25. Wright to William A. Hulbert, Dec. 29, 1874. Wright Correspondence, VI. Chadwick, Scrapbooks, I, 99. Wright, Note and Account Books, II.

26. Spalding, *America's National Game,* pp. 200–207. *New York Clipper,* Dec. 25, 1875.

27. Wright to Hulbert, Dec. 29, 1874, Wright Correspondence, VI.

5

The Chicago Black Sox and the myth of baseball's single sin*

Forthcoming rites celebrating major league baseball's centennial season will draw heavily from gilded myths perpetuated by sportswriting troubadors. Despite the iconoclastic spirit of our age, the fairy-tale quality of our baseball legends persists. Perhaps the escapist world of the sports page with its colorful and stylized prose is the best environment for sheltering and nurturing myths—particularly two of the most persistent: the "immaculate conception myth" that professional baseball began in Cincinnati in 1869, and the "single sin myth" that only once has corruption tainted the game. That episode was the Chicago White Sox scandal of 1919.

A brief recap of the first of these myths is necessary for our understanding of the second, which is our chief concern. Apparently the immaculate conception theory is baseball's favorite way of explaining the appearance of its institutions. Despite abundant evidence showing that many players received money for their services before 1869, the official myth

*First published in *Journal of the Illinois State Historical Society,* Vol. 62, No. 3 (Autumn, 1969). Slightly revised.

credits the Cincinnati Reds of that year with inventing the professional game by fielding the first paid team. When the Reds went undefeated for so long, this inspired the immaculate conception in 1871 of the first professional league, the National Association.[1] This league lasted five years until its instability forced it to yield to another immaculate conception, the National League—a result of a coup promoted by Chicagoan William A. Hulbert and Albert Spalding. Then, after more than a quarter of a century of National League dominance, baseball legend reports the immaculate conception of the present dual major league system. After a brief war ending in 1903, the American League joined forces with the older National League to create a structural pattern for big league baseball that lasted until 1969 when the present four divisional pattern appeared.[2]

So heavy a reliance on the immaculate conception myth to explain pragmatic evolutionary developments helps to explain why American baseball leaders came to feel a divinely guided sense of mission. Since the game was destined to be America's national game, its apologists believed that only flagrant dishonesty could thwart the divine plan.[3]

The myth of baseball's single sin states that the game's promise was thwarted by the 1919 World Series scandal, which had been two years in the brewing. Back in 1914, desperate for a championship after eight years of drought,[4] owner Charles Comiskey of the White Sox began purchasing star players. In 1915 he bought the hard-hitting outfielder Joe Jackson, and for an unprecedented $140,000 purchased second baseman Eddie Collins to go with the previously acquired trio of pitcher Ed Cicotte, catcher Ray Schalk, and infielder Buck Weaver.[5] The key acquisition was Collins, who became field captain. Although an effective leader, Collins was unpopular with a cabal of players who resented his polish, his authority, and his high salary. Led by first baseman Chick Gandil the clique included Cicotte, Weaver, Jackson, and pitcher Claude "Lefty" Williams. Together they made life miserable for Collins and for manager Clarence Rowland. At the same time, some of their off-field contacts with gamblers portended trouble for the White Sox. But in 1917 these troubles were masked by a world championship which the Sox scored over the National League Giants in the World Series. The following year America's total involvement in war drew attention away from baseball.[6]

With peace restored, by 1919 baseball fortunes were rising sharply. War-weary fans returned in droves, thus restoring old profit patterns; and when Sunday baseball was legalized in New York, an era of greater profits loomed. Given exciting pennant races in 1919, which attracted droves of youthful fans, thousands cheered the Cincinnati Reds on to their first pennant in this century. And despite the bitter summer race riots in Chicago, even larger throngs backed manager William (Kid) Gleason's White Sox as they drove to a hard-fought victory over the challenging Cleveland Indians.[7]

That fall the impending World Series clash of these rivals promised to eclipse all previous attendance records. Although the White Sox were favored, Cincinnati fans took heart when the Reds won the first two games, played in Cincinnati, by 9–1 and 4–2 margins. Moving to Chicago, manager Pat (Whiskey Face) Moran's Reds lost one to Chicago's little left-handed pitching star, Dick Kerr, 3–2, but the Reds rebounded to win the next two by shutout scores of 2–0 and 5–0. Now looking like sure winners and needing but one more win to clinch the nine-game World Series, the Reds trembled as Chicago battled back to win the next two by 5–4 and 4–1 scores. With the last two games scheduled for Chicago and with Claude "Lefty" Williams ready to pitch the first, Chicago fans waxed optimistic. But what followed was a cruel blow: Williams gave up four runs in the first inning, and Chicago went on to lose both the game and the 1919 World Series.[8]

So runs the official account of the 1919 Series; if it had been allowed to rest, it might have ranked the Reds' victory somewhere behind the victory of the "Miracle Braves of 1914" in the annals of underdog victories. That it was not interred was due to persistent rumors telling of gamblers who had paid off some of the White Sox players for losing games. In 1920 the official *Spalding Guide* sniffed at these "rumors of collusion," but editor John B. Foster dismissed them as sour grapes. As Foster saw it, the experts simply had been wrong in failing to gauge the true strength of the Reds, whose superb teamwork was highlighted in the Series by Edd Roush's lusty hitting and by the pitching of Dutch Reuther, "Slim" Sallee, and Jim Ring.[9] But the rumors would not be stilled. And baseball fans heard that Ray Schalk, the heroic White Sox catcher, had goaded Cicotte and Williams with obscenities matched in eloquence only by those of his manager. Indeed, fans of the Cincinnati Reds were talking about manager Moran's asking pitcher Hod Eller if gamblers had gotten to him. "Yep," Eller replied, and cheerfully admitted refusing a $5,000 bribe. Shocked by Eller's candor, Moran allowed him to pitch but watched him carefully as Eller won easily.[10]

Had the rumors been confined to the playing field, the player code of "speak no evil" before outsiders would probably have preserved the official version of the lost 1919 Series games. But that fall the continuing rumors attracted the attention of Hugh Fullerton, a popular syndicated sportswriter. To a prying reporter like Fullerton, tracking rumors was the joy of life. His sleuthing helped to uncover the tangled tales of corruption that made the real story of the 1919 Series an American morality play. In lifting the lid on the Pandora's box, Fullerton was assisted by the great pitcher Christy Mathewson, who was doing feature stories on the Series for the *New York World*. No stranger to the seamy side of baseball, "Matty" was honestly worried about crookedness in the game. Hence, he became Fullerton's expert adviser and provided the reporter with diagrams of each questionable play in the Series games.[11] With these diagrams and with his own findings, Fullerton wrote a series of sensational articles telling of a fix, the fixers, and their ill-gotten gains.

Although widely read, the articles were generally discounted, one critic sneering that Fullerton was "always scoffing at the honesty of an institution, no matter how sacred." [12] Nevertheless, Fullerton's darts spurred four independent investigations as National League president John Heydler, American League president Johnson, Bill Veeck (Sr.) of the Cubs, and Comiskey each hired detectives to check out the rumors. Comiskey even offered $10,000 as a reward for bona fide proof of corruption.[13]

At this point there was a chance the thing might blow over—a whirlwind lost amid gales of evil. After all, Americans of 1919 were daily reminded of bigger evils such as the Bolshevik threat and the threat of left-wing intellectuals, labor leaders, and sundry dissenters—all avidly pursued by patriotic witchhunters. Other stories told of looting in Boston in the wake of a police strike. And the year 1920 produced more lurid headlines about smuggling rings carrying booze for the revolt of American drinkers against national prohibition. In August there was also the exposé of stock swindler Charles Ponzi, a former convict who bilked $5 million from investors with a naive stock-jobbing scheme.[14]

Notwithstanding all the stiff competition, news from the 1920 baseball campaign kept the rumor pot boiling. While Brooklyn coasted to an easy victory in the National League, the American League had a lively three-way race among Chicago, Cleveland, and New York. Before the season ended, fans read of Babe Ruth's home runs and the tragic death of the Cleveland shortstop Ray Chapman, who was killed by a wild pitch. Chapman's death made Cleveland the sentimental favorite of American league fans, and the team outlasted the White Sox by two games.[15] The victory deserved celebration as a triumph of courage, but late-breaking news of more Chicago corruption sullied the Cleveland achievement.

Certainly a smart baseball man like Comiskey might have known that unpunished corruption breeds more corruption. For an agonizing period in 1919, he had considered not releasing the extra salary checks for World Series play to his suspected players, and he delayed mailing them their 1920 contracts.

In the end, to his lasting regret, he did both, thereby encouraging more dishonesty. Thus, late in the 1920 season new rumors told of some of his men receiving payoffs for losing key games, possibly enough to allow Cleveland to win. Game selling soon spread beyond Comiskey Park; and before the season ended infielder Lee Magee of the crosstown Cubs was fired for attempting to fix a game with the Phillies.[16]

By September all these tales were generally known along with those of the 1919 Series. Drastic action was needed to save the majors from charges that gamblers were running the entire show. In mid-September, baseball faced a Cook County grand jury investigation into the 1919 scandal allegations. Hard after this came James Isaminger's story in the *Philadelphia North American*, based on an interview with gambler Bill Maharg, who supplied details of the fix and the names of the fixers. As the story broke, the 1920 White Sox were only a game and a half out of first place, and at that point pitcher Ed Cicotte and infielder George "Buck" Weaver confessed to Comiskey. Angrily, Comiskey told both to go to the grand jury; and then he suspended the eight players whom all along he had known to be guilty. Comiskey thereby lost the services of the best players he ever had as well as the 1920 pennant. Beyond this he was unmasked as one who put personal profit ahead of integrity, for now he stood guilty of remaining silent in the face of suspected corruption. The consequences of his dilatory action were far reaching; by undermining the prestige of American League president Ban Johnson, Comiskey also undermined baseball's national commission system of rule. As a result, in 1921 the commission was replaced by a single commissioner, Judge Kenesaw Mountain Landis, whose theatrically stern rulings over a twenty-five-year period gave baseball a proper image of decorum—thereby reinstating the myth of the game's single sin.[17]

The rest of the dismal story is well known, although its bizarre details yet defy understanding. Eight men from

Comiskey's White Sox were branded as "Black Sox," including the great Joe Jackson, owner of a .356 lifetime batting average;[18] pitchers Cicotte and Williams; infielders Weaver, Gandil (who retired from the game early in 1920), and Charles "Swede" Risberg; and outfielders Oscar "Happy" Felsch and utility man Fred McMullin.[19]

Facing the grand jury, Cicotte tearfully told of getting $10,000, which he used to pay off a farm mortgage; Jackson testified that he got only $5,000 of a promised $20,000. Williams told the grand jury that gamblers had threatened to kill his wife unless he let down in the final game. All agreed that Gandil, who had received $35,000 in bribery, was the instigator and chief profiteer. According to later testimony, Cicotte admitted to making still more money by betting on the Reds to win the fixed games. Only Weaver said he got nothing, and he insisted that he had pulled out of the conspiracy but agreed to shut up about it.[20]

Naturally the real winners were the gamblers. The grand jury managed to smoke out the "king of gamblers," Arnold Rothstein, who appeared as a friendly witness and named Abe Attell as the chief conspirator, himself disclaiming any part in the intrigue. Much later, after spending $10,000 of American League funds for a private investigation, Johnson in July 1921 accused Rothstein of a more active role. Although the charge was libelous, Rothstein refused to sue, perhaps acting on the advice of a colleague who once cautioned, "Never sue. They might prove it." [21]

In June 1921, a conspiracy trial was held in Chicago before Judge Hugo Friend. It was only a farce, however, since the records of the grand jury and the confessions of Cicotte, Jackson, and Williams had mysteriously disappeared. Another bizarre development, it enabled the eight players to repudiate their confessions. Hopelessly crippled by lack of evidence, and confronted by a jury friendly to the players, the trial turned into a comic carnival. The trial ended on August 2, and the "not guilty" verdict brought cheers from the spectators, some of whom shouted, "Hooray for the Clean

Sox." [22] But if judged innocent under civil law, the eight were found guilty under baseball law. The final arbiter was commissioner Landis and as sole executioner he summarily barred all eight from baseball for life.[23] For the rest of their lives the eight players wore the stigma of "Black Sox," and in spite of repeated appeals, Landis stubbornly refused to grant a single pardon.

To protest this arbitrary judgment on any grounds is to run a twofold risk: that of undermining one of baseball's most sanctimonious myths and that of awakening the ghost of Landis. Yet the fact is that the players were denied their civil rights by the application of baseball law. Today such a ruling could never happen lest it evoke a heavy lawsuit; and even in 1921 its imposition was a legal error, resting on the moral consensus of baseball owners who were supported by the general public—all apparently unaware of the implications for civil liberties but overaware of their own pious definitions of sin and evil.

Those harried baseball Ishmaels lived furtive lives. Shunned by organized baseball, they were thwarted in any attempts to ply their trade. Some occasionally caught on with semiprofessional or outlaw leagues who played them under aliases, but exposure inevitably led to pressure which ousted them. Only Buck Weaver fought on with head high. He sued in the courts and won a partial payment on his 1920 contract. Six times he appealed to Landis for reinstatement, once armed with a petition bearing 14,000 signatures, but each time he was rebuffed. Jackson tried playing under assumed names until he could no longer bear the pain of exposure.[24] In 1969 Cicotte died, after living for some years under an assumed name, yet later proud of a relative whom he coached and who made the majors under the Cicotte name. And in 1971 Gandil died; four months before he had vowed, "I'll go to my grave with a clear conscience." Yet he was dead ten weeks before word reached the *New York Times*.[25] Of the unfortunate lot only Swede Risberg remains alive.

To understand why the eight men recklessly gambled their

reputations on this ill-conceived intrigue is to probe the dark side of the human condition. They played on a clique-ridden team which pitted a sophisticated group, led by Collins, against their own earthy, boorish group, led by Gandil. Jealousy and verbal abuse marked the infighting as Gandil's faction attacked Collins' "dudish" manners and his $15,000 salary. Since none of the Gandil faction made over $6,000, this group continually groused about Comiskey's cheapness, and, indeed, his 1919 payroll was one of baseball's lowest.[26]

The argument is spurious which says being underpaid gives license to cheat, and so is the argument that many wrongs make a right. But the Black Sox did have a point in using such defenses. The myth of baseball's single sin proclaims that the game has known but one case of proven dishonesty, yet the early years of the game were pockmarked with countless rumors of bribery and cheating similar to this episode. In 1877 a clique of Louisville players was expelled for selling games, and shortly thereafter an umpire was ousted for dishonesty.[27] In the first modern World Series, played in 1903, catcher Lou Criger reportedly rejected a $12,000 bribe, and in the second Rube Waddell was offered $17,000 not to play. Coincidentally or not, he injured himself falling over a suitcase and did not appear.[28] There were rumors of fixed games in the 1918 Series, and evidence of fixers centered about the victorious Reds of 1919. Outfielder Edd Roush later related that one suspected plotter got on base accidentally. To score would threaten the fix, so the player lagged on Roush's long hit that followed, but hot on his heels Roush goaded him to score, shouting, "Get running, you crooked son of a bitch."[29]

Still other blotches spattered baseball's image. In 1908 some Phillies threw a gambler down the clubhouse stairs at the Polo Grounds after he offered them a bribe.[30] With a torrid pennant race that ended in a tie, that same season found umpires Bill Klem and Charles Johnson reporting a bribe attempt in behalf of the Giants in their playoff game with the Cubs.[31] And in 1916 the Giants were accused of lying down to help the Dodgers beat the Phillies—a charge

Giant manager John McGraw thought to be true.[32] Meanwhile persistent rumors of game selling centered about Hal Chase of the Giants. Inquiry into the Black Sox case dredged up evidence that Chase and Joe Gedeon of the Browns had made money betting on the Reds. By dragging their feet in the 1919 investigation, baseball men thus created a climate favoring more corruption in 1920. That year detectives found evidence linking two Giants and four Cubs with fix plots, and cast suspicion on some Yankees, Braves, Red Sox, and Indians players. No mere rumors these, for they led directly to the blacklisting of Magee and pitcher Claude Hendrix of the Cubs.[33]

These are but documented incidents in a record of sporadic dishonesty extending through baseball history. A well-established, though clearly unethical, baseball practice of the time was the quaint custom whereby a contending ball club offered a suit of clothes to a noncontending pitcher for beating another contender; the custom sometimes had variations as in 1917 when the White Sox awarded suits to Detroit players for losing two doubleheaders.[34] In 1921 Landis sternly ordered such practices stopped.

After two decades of holding their noses and indoctrinating newsmen with the myth of the incorruptible national game, baseball men at last made scapegoats of the most brazen cheaters. But they did not purge one of their own for withholding evidence that might have cleaned house in 1919 and possibly headed off the 1920 scandals.[35] To save his own investment, Charles Comiskey had stood silent in the face of corruption. Knowing this, his colleagues isolated him after 1920. His last years were sick and lonely ones; his one consolation was that he kept his franchise.

In retrospect, the year 1920 was not a time for casting first stones. What Landis, the players, and fans seemingly sensed was that notions of sin were changing in a get-rich-quick, fast-buck America. Apparently the fans could overlook revealed corruption, for they kept coming, enabling the American League to top the 5 million attendance mark in 1920.

Moreover, in spite of screaming scandal headlines about Black Sox, the 1920 Series drew well.[36]

Had they kept cool under the fire of angry headlines and probing investigators, baseball leaders might have wielded power as of old. But they panicked, and a majority voted to bring in a famous outsider as commissioner to lend the game an honest image; the era of Judge Landis began in 1920 and lasted until 1944. By cleverly playing the role of "puritan in Babylon," Landis convinced most fans that baseball's "guilty season" was over. True, there were continuing scandals, but the Judge singled out enough scapegoats to keep baseball's reputation intact and the players cowed. As old Dan Cassidy, Cicotte's attorney in 1920, recently put it; "The players had no organization then. Now they do. This sort of thing couldn't happen today."[37] Largely then, through Landis's efforts, the myth of baseball's single sin is alive today.

NOTES

1. Voigt, "America's First Red Scare," pp. 13–24.
2. Voigt, *American Baseball* (1966), pp. 39–40, 60–79, 99–120.
3. Spalding, *America's National Game,* pp. 3–14. Spalding gives the classic statement of baseball's mission; for modern utterances of this sort, see excerpts from commissioner Bowie Kuhn's speech, *New York Times,* April 10, 1969, p. 57.
4. Leonard Gettelson, *Official World Series Records* (St. Louis, 1965), p. 251.
5. G. W. Axelson, *"Commy": The Life Story of Charles A. Comiskey* (Chicago: Reilly and Lee, 1919), pp. 202–3.
6. *Ibid.,* pp. 214–16.
7. *Ibid.,* pp. 216–18.
8. Gettelson, *Official World Series Records,* pp. 54–56.
9. Spalding's *Official Baseball Guide, 1920,* pp. 5–15.
10. Lawrence S. Ritter, *The Glory of Their Times* (New York, 1966), pp. 214–15.
11. Eliot Asinof, *Eight Men Out: The Black Sox and the 1919 World Series* (New York, 1963), pp. 46–47.
12. *Baseball Magazine,* Dec., 1920.
13. Asinof, *Eight Men,* pp. 199–200.
14. Laurence Greene, *The Era of Wonderful Nonsense: A Casebook of the Twenties* (New York: Bobbs Merrill, 1939), pp. 52–53.
15. Gettelson, *Official World Series Records,* pp. 57–58.
16. Asinof, *Eight Men,* pp. 143–44.

17. *Ibid.,* pp. 132–74.
18. Murray Olderman, *Encyclopedia of Baseball* (New York: Nelson, 1963), p. 550.
19. *New York Times,* Sept. 29, 1920, p. 1.
20. *Ibid.*
21. Asinof, *Eight Men,* pp. 258–59.
22. *Chicago Daily Tribune,* Aug. 3, 1921, p. 1.
23. Asinof, *Eight Men,* p. 273.
24. *Ibid.,* pp. 280–92; interview with James T. Farrell, 1967.
25. *New York Times,* May 10, 1969, p. 31 (Cicotte's obituary); Feb. 26, 1971 (Gandil's obituary); *Sporting News,* Sept. 6, 1969 (Gandil interview).
26. Asinof, *Eight Men,* pp. 18, 20. *Baseball Magazine,* March 1916; made this remarkable prophecy concerning Joe Jackson: "Wait five years or so. Then Joe will go through all he had made in baseball and will be broke once more. What will he do? Why go back in the cotton mill . . . for $1.25."
27. Asinof, *Eight Men,* pp. 11–12.
28. *Ibid.,* p. 207.
29. Interview with James T. Farrell, 1967. See also William Veeck, Jr., and Ed Linn, *The Hustler's Handbook* (New York, 1965), pp. 252–99.
30. Asinof, *Eight Men,* p. 207.
31. *Baseball Magazine,* Nov. 1908, pp. 11–12.
32. Fred Lieb and Stan Baumgartner, *The Philadelphia Phillies* (New York, 1953), p. 139.
33. Veeck and Linn, *Hustler's Handbook,* pp. 252–99.
34. *Ibid.,* p. 274.
35. *Sporting News,* Nov. 4, 1920.
36. Gettelson, *Official World Series Records,* p. 58.
37. David Q. Voigt, "Kenesaw M. Landis, *Dictionary of American Biography; New York Times,* Aug. 16, 1969.

BALL 3

Baseball—mirror of American life

A major promise of the study of sports is insight into the structure of society. The century long history of major league baseball fulfills this promise by shedding light on many of the changing themes and structures in American social life. Of the following quartet of essays, two focus on the development of the American nation, showing the rise of American nationalism and its accompanying theme of continuing manifest destiny. A third essay probes the changing structure of American society and challenges the myth of the melting pot. That baseball mirrors the growing tendency of our citizens to cluster into veto groups in hopes of securing the blessings of democratic life is the theme of the final essay.

6

American baseball and American nationalism

Once one grasps the broad historical outline of a sport like major league baseball, one's imagination turns up endless leads for exploring the connections between stages of baseball history and their counterparts in American life, particularly insights into our elusive national character. To follow these leads is hopefully to gain a better understanding of what being an American has meant, now means, and may come to mean.

To begin is to explore the idea of nationalism, that driving theme which over the past century has altered the institutions of our society. Because American nationalism is linked with the rise of our great spectator sports and vice versa, the sports historian need not fear to probe this domain of intellectual history. An excellent stimulus to one's historical imagination is Arthur O. Lovejoy's book, *Essays in the History of Ideas*. Lovejoy offers assurances that ideas, after all, are manmade catchwords that change over time yet are seldom really new; that historians of ideas are not geniuses, but rather bold individualists who dislike teamwork; and that an idea can be expected to crop up in almost any avenue of thought.[1]

A powerful, motivating idea, modern nationalism arose out of that bubbling cauldron of the restive eighteenth century when percolating ideologies of the Enlightenment were boiling away the old church and sovereignty models of control. As kings lost power and were swept aside, so too went the power of churchmen; Enlightenment political philosophy held up the model of the secular nation state as a proper unit of social organization. By the end of that century at least five versions of the idea of nationalism were operating in Europe. As described by the late Carlton J. H. Hayes, they included an *humanitarian* form with an emphasis on man's potential goodness, to be brought out by the diffusion of reason and science. Opposing this gradualist model of utopian reform was *Jacobin* nationalism. Inspired by the French Revolution, it prescribed violence, extremism, terrorism, and militarism as the formula for the speedy revamping of social orders. By advocating the overthrow of traditional institutions and by its elevating of men like Robespierre and Napoleon, this style stiffened the resistance of another, *traditional* nationalism. Embedded in this idea was the image of a state as a continuing chain of past, present, and future generations of people. Bitterly opposed to rapid social change, its advocates outlawed all revolution, except in rare cases of "legitimate" revolts against a regime which had departed from its traditional obligations.

But most appealing to Americans was the *liberal* nationalistic style with its emphasis on individual freedom, on limited government, and on *laissez faire* economic policies. So broadly appealing was this style in America, that our politicians long dreamed of exporting it everywhere in hopes of ushering in a global millenium of peace and economic prosperity. That so far this has been a forlorn hope may be due to weaknesses with the ideology itself, for its very defense of free competition tends to foment rivalry and envy. Thus, as nations lost out in the competitive scramble for riches, their leaders held up a fifth style of nationalism, *integral* nationalism. A grimly familiar model of this style was advanced by Adolph Hitler, who repressed liberal nationalism in Germany and called on all Germans to put national self-interest and tribal egoism first.[2] As World War II taught, the confrontation between the two nationalist styles was bloody indeed; nor are its by-products of brutality, racism, and bloodshed absent from our world.

That Americans are by no means immune to the unifying promise of integral nationalism is a sober and chilling thought that becomes even more frightening when one reads of recent opinion polls showing a blasé public attitude toward the meaning of the current Watergate episode. Indeed, some writers like Max Lerner see the threat of integral nationalism in our love for mass spectator sports, which he thinks shows us to be a nation of passive onlookers, easily led by charis-matic heroes of the moment.[3]

Be that as it may, as the first new nation, our nationalistic history shows cases in which all five nationalistic styles have appeared. But in the main, liberal nationalism dominated our thought. Emerging in 1789, our new nation was legitimized by the personal charisma of Washington, while the Constitu-tion held out a basis for symbolic unity. Yet not until the Civil War was the Constitution accepted without challenge; prior to the end of that conflict many states and factions tried at various times to destroy the Constitutional union. But the decisive outcome of that war, combined with the conciliatory compromise of 1876 and the great strides in industrialization, rallied the country around liberal nationalist ideologies. And the new style was reflected in the shared values of the people. To be economically independent became a driving quest for individual Americans. And if hard work, frugality, and inita-tive could advance a man, the same values were embraced by groups as a formula for growth. Thus, economic growth and territorial expansion became twin measurements of the worth of individuals and of groups. To score on both counts spelled success; hence, the values of autonomy and free choice became national values, transcending local and subcultural values. True, the future would show how the successful pursuit of such goals raised up large scale organizations which would reduce individuals to corporate workers or other-directed conformists; yet, in the main, the values of autonomy and free choice remain strong to this day.[4]

This driving theme of our post-Civil War culture caught the attention of a generation of American historians who tried in various ways to explain its meaning. Writing in the years following the Civil War, this school of nationalist historians included men like James Ford Rhodes, who narrated the military and political thrust of American nationalism. Others like Charles A. Beard and Matthew Josephson considered its economic impact, and men like John Bach McMaster opened up the realm of social history as a reflector of nationalistic social sentiments.

Certainly liberal nationalism as an integrating social force is reflected in the rising sporting institutions of America. It is a theme writ large in the history of major league baseball, a sport that grew to impressive proportions during the Civil War era. The war helped to diffuse the sport and to popularize it among Americans of all classes; baseball speedily shed its image as an eastern regional sport played by snobbish gentlemen and their muscular mercenaries. Part of the fruit of this rapid growth process was an immediate postwar baseball boom that commercialists quickly exploited. In 1871 a group of opportunistic promoters organized the first commercialized major league in hopes of cashing in on the boom. In so doing they made every effort to press baseball's claim to being America's national game.[5]

That the leading advocate of baseball as our national game was also first to become a millionaire from its successful exploitation was no accident. This was Albert Goodwill Spalding, the young pitcher who as a teenager in 1865 organized and captained the Rockford, Illinois, "Forest City" team, before moving to Boston where he performed as star pitcher for the Red Stocking champions of 1872–75 in the first major league. To popularize the game and to make it pay were Spalding's twin goals. While at Boston, he helped to hatch the notion of sending a baseball mission to Britain in hopes of spreading the American game. And in 1875 he determined that the National Association, with its policy of player control, was counterproductive and must therefore be scuttled. That year he plotted the coup that produced the National League, giving power to the clubowners. Then in 1877 he retired from active play to manufacture sports equipment and serve as owner of the Chicago White Stockings. An architect of a baseball equipment trust, he drove out all rivals in building a varied, multimillion dollar sporting goods empire. And as a wily National League policy maker, he masterminded the plots that fended off all attempts by players or rival leagues to wrest power from the National League and its "legitimate" owners.

That Spalding succeeded owed much to his shrewd exploitation of baseball's claim to being America's national game. Through his subsidiary, the American Sports Publishing Company, Spalding turned out official guides for nearly every professional league in America and abroad. Throughout the nineteenth century he employed as chief editor the influential Henry Chadwick, who once proclaimed baseball to be "in every way . . . suited to the American character." As a prolific writer and hack editor Chadwick faithfully struck this note for two score years, constantly persuading lesser writers, a cliché-ridden lot who looked to Chadwick as their dean, to pick up the tune. Thus, baseball as America's national game—our invention by immaculate conception—became one of the most hackneyed phrases of that age. That writers and fans came to believe the myth owed much to Spalding's efforts. Tirelessly he plugged the game as "our national game," and in 1905 he financed the historical commission that found Cooperstown to be the Bethlehem of baseball. Thus came the Abner Doubleday myth with its magical date of 1839 for the game's founding. In 1911, three years after Chadwick's death,

Spalding drew upon that faithful servant's notes and records to publish *America's National Game*, at the time the most complete and also the most chauvinistic history of American baseball. The nationalistic rhetoric and myth includes an unforgettable alliterative piece proclaiming baseball to the American people as "the exponent of American Courage, Confidence, Combatism; American Dash, Discipline, Determinism; American Energy, Eagerness, Enthusiasm; American Pluck, Persistency, Performance; American Spirit, Sagacity, Success; American Vim, Vigor, Virility. . . ." Also included was Spalding's acceptance of that tired coaching myth from which our age is just beginning to disenthrall itself; as Spalding put it, "baseball gives . . . a growing boy self-poise and self-reliance. Baseball is a man maker." [6]

By such zealous promotion the myth of American baseball as our national sport found its way into the mainstream of American folklore. Yet those who dance to nationalist tunes must pay the piper. Thus, promoters while manipulating American nationalistic sentiments to serve their interests were themselves buffeted by the same driving force, a reminder to all of the truth of the adage, that he who sows the wind reaps the whirlwind.

For openers, baseball men, in pandering to the political forces that gave shaky organization to the sentiment of American nationalism, found themselves in thrall to political manipulators. This became clear as soon as baseball leaders sought recognition of their sport from American Presidents. This came as early as 1869 when President Grant met with the members of the Cincinnati Red Stocking team and complimented them on their fine play. Later Cap Anson's Chicago White Stockings got to shake hands with President Cleveland, at which time each player sought to outdo another by squeezing Cleveland's hand as hard as he could. And when President Taft agreed to throw out the first ball of the Washington Senators' opening day game, an annual Washington custom was launched which guaranteed the lowly Senators at least one paying crowd a year. Each subsequent incident of Presidential recognition confirmed baseball's status; yet each exacted its cost. Recent baseball's payoff required baseball men to accommodate an image-conscious President like Nixon, providing him a chance to boost his political stock by appearing on dramatic occasions like the World Series to be photographed in the company of winners. It also means that baseball must vote Republican or Democratic according to the direction of political wins. Also if a Nixon desired to enhance his jock image by naming his personal all-time baseball all-star team, and by lacing his rhetoric with "sportspeak," baseball men must stand by approvingly, leaving criticism of Nixon to prickly reporters like Red Smith, who, sniffing at Nixon's 2,800 word, cliché-filled essay on baseball immortals (that Smith said should have been completed in 800), welcomed the President as "the new slow boy on the baseball beat."[7]

Nor are representatives of other political institutions shy about using baseball. In exploring baseball's link with urban politics, Steven Riess has shown that between 1900 and 1920 sixteen major league clubs forged links with local politicos, a burden equal to that carried by Jacob Marley.[8] And in 1920, when the Supreme Court granted major league baseball immunity from antitrust prosecution (an interesting nationalistic concession in itself), subject to Congressional concurrence, baseball officials found themselves thrice obliged to turn over their secret files to the scrutiny of Congressman Emmanuel Celler's investigative subcommittee; each time the printed revelations delighted baseball historians hungry for inside data, although national regulative legislation has not yet been forthcoming.

In other ways national politics has bent baseball to its purposes. For example, an important element of American nationalism is our pride in our military prowess, a sentiment backed by pressure on groups to do honor to those who wield arms. Over the years this has been a repetitive and continuing obligation, as evidenced by those sociological studies comparing our society with other modern states in the number of years spent at war. It was found that America ranks near the top for having spent more time at war since 1860. Not surprisingly, it has become baseball's ongoing task to support every war, from that imperialist struggle with Spain that John Hay called "a splendid little war," through two World Wars, and most recently two peace-keeping conflicts—all expressing a missionary aspect of American nationalism. For its part, baseball gained chauvinistic recognition for its morale-boosting, which enhanced its claim to being the national game. But in return, baseball men felt obliged to supply military camps with bats and balls, to admit servicemen free to games, to broadcast war news over loudspeaker systems, and on occasion to have players derided for being "slackers." Indeed, on two occasions, in 1918 and in 1945, the game narrowly missed being closed down by zealous war secretaries who toyed with the notion of using ballparks as military storage depots.[9] Meanwhile the era between the two great wars saw the rise of a potent veterans group, the American Legion. As a pressure group, the Legion has kept Congresses and Presidents ever alert to military and patriotic needs, as defined by Legion spokesmen. And because the Legion has also sponsored a national youth baseball program, regarded as an important source of major league player talent, the game's leaders seem to feel it prudent to conform to the Legion's definitions of patriotism.

Fresh in our minds is the long Vietnam struggle, pronounced in 1973 to be ended with "peace with honor." Although many Americans opposed our involvement, baseball leaders could not join the peace movements, and when a player like Tug McGraw did speak up at a dinner, he felt the chill of official disapproval. Also, to help foster the peace with honor rhetoric, the 1973 opening day ceremonies, largely at Nixon's instigation, featured freed prisoners of war throwing out first balls. This was another reminder of the game's obligation to support the litany of peace with honor while ignoring hard won lessons that Vietnam may have held.

From an esthetic point of view the highest price baseball

may have paid in securing its image as America's national game may have been an obligation to play our national anthem at each game. The custom has a curious history. Owing to sectional bickering no national anthem existed until, at the outbreak of the first World War, President Wilson decreed that the "Star Spangled Banner" should serve. Major league clubs fell into line that year, and, while lacking public address systems, hired bands to play the tune. After the war the custom lingered, although the tune was heard only at World Series games or other dates such as patriotic holidays. But in 1931 Congress finally voted to institutionalize the "Star Spangled Banner" as our national anthem, and Hoover signed it into law in March. From then on, using newly developed loudspeaker systems, the tune was heard on opening days and at World Series games. Only with the coming of World War II did the custom of playing and singing the tune at every game take hold. Perhaps it seems longer to those who judge the quality of the tune unsingable, chanting. Yet Americans, including baseball fans and partisans of professional basketball, football and hockey, seem to love their ugly duckling. When Jose Feliciano, the blind guitarist, essayed a Puerto-Rican soul version of the anthem at Detroit in a 1968 World Series game, his revitalizing efforts drew hot criticism and some charges of subversion. And in June 1972 when Ewing Kauffman, owner of the Kansas City Royals, attempted to limit the playing of the national anthem, he held out only two days before some 200 complaints persuaded him to penitently restore the custom. Thus does American baseball retard musical virtuosity by serving the cause of patriotism! Perhaps a glimmer of hope for improvement lies in the presence of the Montreal Expos of the National League. When this Canadian team plays in the States, protocol requires the host club to play both the "Star Spangled Banner" and "O Canada." Perhaps hearing how much we suffer by comparison might persuade fans to lead a movement for a better anthem.[10]

The seamy side of American nationalist sentiments is also

mirrored in American baseball history. Nationalistic historians agree that one of the essential compromises of our post-
Civil War national unity came in 1876 when the Republican
party accepted a disputed Presidency in return for permitting
the South and the rest of the nation to handle problems of
black Americans locally. In the repression of blacks under
Jim Crow customs that followed, we glimpse the dark side of
our nationalism—a reminder of the truth of Professor Hayes'
warning that America, too, has its examples of integral nationalism with its themes of group superiority. For its part
American baseball followed this social-Darwinian siren call
slavishly. In 1882 the Walker brothers were barred from the
major leagues, followed later by Lou Nava and a scattering
of others. In his autobiography Captain Adrian Anson of the
Chicago White Stockings admitted to leading the drive to
whitewash major league baseball. His influence hastened the
lowering of a Jim Crow curtain lasting until after World War
II. During that war, the rhetoric of liberty and equality
forced changes in our norms and American baseball was
obliged to catch up with more progressive sports in expiating
a longstanding wrong. This baseball leaders did, but with
much deceptive puffery and much inconsistency, as studies
of this aspect of baseball have pointed out. And baseball's
foot-dragging mirrors similar patterns of resistance to integration in other social institutions. Today tension between
black and white in baseball continues, complicated by variations on the theme such as tension between American
players and Latin Americans. Such examples testify to a continuing acceptance by Americans of group superiority beliefs.
As such it must be regarded as part of our national character.

Even more transcendent than our acceptance of group superiority as a theme is our acceptance of growth as a necessity. According to Professor Lipset the two essential elements
of the American style of nationalism are the shared values of
industrial growth and of territorial expansion. According to
Lipset, these values transcend all subcultural difference in
their near unanimous acceptance. Both goad Americans to

act.[11] To most Americans, the life of any individual or group is successful when its activities increase its wealth or territory. And in American baseball the pursuit of these twin goals looms large. Over the past century baseball leaders never failed to celebrate rising profits, whirring turnstiles, increasing exposure through multimedia, and expanding territory, as measured by the locating of new franchises in profitable urban areas. Beginning in the 1950s and continuing to this day, baseball leaders boldly pursued a horsehide version of manifest destiny, first leading to a coast-to-coast baseball empire, and, with the recent acquisition of Montreal, now leading to the claimed status of a multinational corporation. Nor is there any abatement in the expansionist sentiment of baseball promoters. It can be fairly stated that the future as envisioned by such promoters sees franchises in Mexico, Latin America, Japan, and Taiwan as part of a dream of Christmas-yet-to-come.

That such a dream may have dysfunctional implications seems not to have troubled baseball leaders, who apparently believe their own propaganda. Yet it would seem that in mounting the steed of nationalism, American baseball has been run away with! To undertake the task of pointing up the dangers in such policies is a duty of sports historians, who most certainly will not be thanked for their efforts. On the whole the results may show that the costs of uncritical embracing of nationalism outweigh the benefits. Certainly, baseball leaders have been forced into a garrison mentality— forever defending their claim to being the American sport against the counterclaims of rivals such as professional football and basketball. Indeed, aside from fending off unionist activity among major league players, this seems to be Commissioner Bowie Kuhn's chief occupation. By no means is it an easy task, because poll after recent poll shows rival sports to be more appealing to fans than baseball.[12]

If being America's national game requires baseball officials to stand by while clever politicos exploit the game for image advantages or for support of military policies, surely this must alienate from baseball those fans who see this posture as pandering to superpatriots and war lovers. Also, what does a true believer in the baseball-as-national-game myth do with the problem of rationalizing the mighty presence of so many black and Latin-American superstars in major league uniforms? What does this do to notions of white supremacy? Certainly it raises the question of how baseball's claim to being the national game can be sustained when its best performing players are alienated from the mainstream of national participation. Beyond these questions looms a larger one—Can a pluralistic society like ours have a national anything? I think that trying to be national in our kind of cultural clime is a millstone about the neck of the game that tries. Once hung on your neck a millstone drags you down. Thus, baseball today seems ever to be defending, rather than advancing or attacking. This might well be the hour for baseball men to abdicate their nationalistic claims before the absurdity of such claims is too far gone.

NOTES

1. Arthur O. Lovejoy, *Essays in the History of Ideas* (New York: G. P. Putnam's Sons, 1960), pp. 1–13.

2. Carleton J. H. Hayes, *Historical Evolution of Modern Nationalism* (New York: Macmillan, 1948), especially pp. 162–63.

3. Max Lerner, *America as a Civilization* (New York: Simon and Schuster, 1957), pp. 818–19.

4. Seymour M. Lipset, *The First New Nation* (New York: Doubleday Anchor Books, 1967), pp. 21, 38, 65–76, 101–11, 145, 162–63, 288.

5. *Harper's Weekly,* Oct. 15, 1859; Nov. 5, 1859; Aug. 31, 1861. This journal carried a debate on whether baseball or "free for all" football ought to be considered as our national game.

6. Arthur Bartlett, *Baseball and Mr. Spalding: The History and Romance of Baseball* (New York: Farrar, Straus and Young, 1951), pp. 2, 11, 27, 37, 289–90.

7. Red Smith, "New Slow Boy on Baseball Beat," *New York Times,* July 3, 1972; "Spoken Like a True Son of Old Whittier," April 30, 1973.

8. Steven Riess, "The Baseball Magnate and Urban Politics, 1895–1923." Paper read before 1973 meeting of North American Society for Sport History, May 26, 1973, Ohio State University.

9. Major league baseball's experiences in three wars are treated in

Voigt's *American Baseball* (1966), pp. 264–66; *American Baseball* (1970), pp. 120–24; 257–69.

10. Phone conversation, April 30, 1973, with Jack Redding, librarian of Baseball Library, Cooperstown, N. Y. See also *Sporting News,* April 19, 1917; Oct. 19, 1968. For recent discussion of the anthem in sports see *New York Times,* Jan. 16, 1973.

11. Lipset, *First New Nation,* pp. 65–67.

12. *New York Times,* Nov. 22, 1967; July 23, 1969. A *Times* poll of April 22, 1973, shows baseball outstripped in public preference by horse racing and football with basketball and hockey in close pursuit. See also Joseph Durso, "What's Happened to Baseball," *Saturday Review,* Sept. 14, 1968; David Halberstam, "Baseball and the National Mythology," *Harper's,* Sept. 1970.

7

American baseball and the mission of America

An internationalist theme of American nationalism is likewise reflected in the century old history of major league baseball. In probing baseball history for reflections of this aspect of our national character one finds solid support for historian Ralph Gabriel's contention that "the mission of America" myth has been and continues to be a major part of our national character. Briefly defined, the myth expresses an act of faith that holds American culture to be so perfect that its major elements ought to be exported so that all peoples of the world might gain by conforming to our system. Tracing our missionary efforts in pursuit of this anthropologically hopeless quest shows our many efforts to save the world by our example. In a violent form this spirit emerges in our manifest destiny adventures of 1846 and 1898, and some might add of the 1960s. Otherwise our zeal has us trying to export constitutional democracy, mixed capitalism, and pan-Christian morality to the world at large.[1] That the myth persists is evidenced in such present-day projects as NATO, the Vietnam

War, the Peace Corps, the multinational corporations, and the Hilton Hotels in so many world capitals—each bearing witness to our lingering dream of wanting to make the world like us.

An athletic expression of this myth is reflected in the history of major league baseball. Three times over the years 1874–1914 baseball promoters launched missionary efforts aimed at planting our game on foreign soils. The first of these ventures came soon after the first major league was launched as baseball promoters, ever pursuing cash and glory, elected to try to export the game to Britain. The idea was a brainchild of Harry Wright, the father of professional baseball, whose pioneering in league organization, rules, strategy and tactics, and club management successfully set up the National Association as a major league and made his Boston Red Stockings its most powerful team. The British-born son of a cricket professional, Wright switched to American baseball, and was impressed by the ease with which the new game replaced cricket in America. It led him to think that British sportsmen would, if they saw baseball played at its best, undergo the same conversion.

Early in 1874 Wright enlisted Albert G. Spalding, his star pitcher, but also a young man driven by ambition to seek a fortune in sporting goods manufacturing, to go to England to treat with the British clubs and to arrange a baseball tour among them. Encouraged by Spalding's claims of success, Wright persuaded the Philadelphia Athletics to join the tour and compete with the Boston team in playing the games in England. It was agreed that the two clubs would share expenses, profits, and glory. A six-week tour was arranged and the two teams departed in the middle of the 1874 season, a move made possible by the lack of a fixed playing schedule under the Association.

Arriving in England in July, the first American baseball mission, with its retinue of players and sportswriters, soon learned that their hosts were more interested in the seven cricket exhibitions that Spalding had been forced to accept.

Indeed, the baseball exhibitions returned a total of less than $2,000 in receipts from puzzled gatherings. Although the cricket matches attracted more attention, this hardly helped the cause of American baseball. Upon discovering our lack of cricket experience, the British elevens patronizingly allowed the Americans to play eighteen men. Although this enabled the Americans "to win" all seven matches, our lack of style branded us as athletic barbarians. As for baseball, the British sporting press compared it with rounders, conceding the game to be fast and scientific, but dismissing it as "the cricket of the American continent." This was far from a conversion and the teams returned home to bask in a whirl of favorable publicity which recouped some of the losses. Although puffed as a success, the mission was a financial and artistic failure.[2]

After this episode, the missionary spirit of baseball promoters slowly revived over the next fourteen years as the fortunes of the major league game rose. Once again it was Spalding who rekindled the spirit. Having successfully engineered the National League coup of 1876, Spalding retired to become a sporting goods entrepreneur. As owner of the famous Chicago White Stockings, by 1888 his was the most powerful voice in National League councils. Ever alert for new markets for his equipment sales, Spalding in 1888 decided to combine his business enterprise with his sense of baseball mission. Recruiting a team of stars called the "All Americans" to compete with his Chicago White Stockings, Spalding arranged an itinerary that would show the game of American baseball in Hawaii, Australia, Egypt, Italy, France, and England.

Cagily, Spalding announced that he did not intend to displace cricket; rather he wanted to establish baseball as a field sport in company with established field sports like cricket and football. Marshalling an efficient staff, Spalding harvested much publicity from enthusiastic sportswriters. Meanwhile his hired publicist, Harry Palmer, prepared Australian and British sportsmen for the coming mission. In Australia copies of Palmer's book, *Base Ball: National Game of the*

Americans,[3] were circulated in advance, proclaiming the primacy of the game in America, supplying its history, a lexicon of its terms, and pictorial ads displaying baseball equipment purchasable at Spalding's new Australian sales outlet.

Spalding's well-oiled mission accommodated players, wives, newspaper men, and staff and left at the close of the 1888 playing season. The first stop, Honolulu, was discouraging to the cause. According to Mark Twain, it was "like interrupting a funeral with a circus." But Australia lifted spirits as fourteen games played at cricket grounds and football fields of Sydney, Melbourne, Adelaide, and some other places drew well and apparently kindled public interest. But elsewhere the games were greeted with mild curiosity often mingled with contempt. In Egypt jeers greeted Spalding's stunt of playing a game near the pyramids, and in Rome an attempt at playing a game in the Colosseum appalled working archeologists, who protested. The Italian government, "scandalized by the suggestion of sacrilege," refused; and when Spalding tried to buy his way in by offering $5,000 to Italian charities, he met a stiffer rebuke.[4] Elsewhere continental reaction was dull, and in England the nine games stirred only slightly more interest than did Wright's tour. Once again British critics dismissed the game, this time calling it a formalized version of rounders, a children's game. When the group returned home, usual welcoming propaganda banquets were dampened by the threat of a players' strike which burst in 1890. Thus ended baseball's second mission—another failure.[5]

Nearly a quarter of a century passed before the next baseball mission was undertaken, years of plaguing domestic problems for major league promoters. Although the game expanded its hold on Americans, economic misfortunes combined with structural problems to make the decade of the 1890s a dismal age for baseball profiteering. But with the restoration of the two major leagues system in 1901 and the revival of World Series competition, public interest and profits increased. By this time competing spectator sports, notably American football and basketball, were vying, challenging baseball's mythbound claim to being America's national game.

On the other hand baseball promoters of 1913 had to be impressed by the stirrings of interest in baseball in other world areas. Reviewing foreign interest in the game in 1910, the *Spalding Guide* counted several Canadian leagues; three leagues and twenty-three teams in Australia; a single league in Johannesburg, South Africa, and promising interest in leagues in Mexico and Central America. But most promising of all was Japan, a land undergoing voluntary and selective Westernization. Baseball had been informally introduced there by American visitors and by student exchanges. By 1909 students at the Japanese universities of Keio and Waseda had hosted a visiting University of Wisconsin team, which dropped three of four games to the Japanese. Since then a surge of Japanese enthusiasm for baseball excited major league promoters into talking up a third mission, with Japan as the chief target for conversion.[6]

Financed by the Spalding interests and by several wealthy owners, the third American baseball mission was led by John McGraw, famous as manager and part owner of the National League New York Giants, and by Charles A. Comiskey, like McGraw a baseball immortal and now owner of the White Sox of the American League. Most of the players were Giants or Chicago White Sox, but some were recruited from other teams. A barnstorming tour of exhibition games helped to finance the venture.

Departing Vancouver in October 1913, the entourage embarked on a 38,000 mile junket with stops at Tokyo, Shanghai, Manila, Melbourne, Cairo, and London as chief ports. As usual a diverse retinue followed in the train, including umpires, newsmen, and a Pathé news photographer. To keep the players in shape during weeks at sea, McGraw and Comiskey held shipboard baseball practice, facilitated by portable screens.

As expected, Japan showed the most interest and the games in Tokyo drew well. Elsewhere interest ranged from modest to poor, but occasionally the presence of political leaders like the Khedive at an Egyptian game, and the King at London, gave a feeling of success.[7] King George V's royal presence tempered some of the London sports critics, one of whom had called the baseball mission a chauvinist plot "to drive out cricket." No doubt the King's presence was a friendly gesture toward a potential ally that would prove helpful in the face of threats of war with Germany. Certainly the King's baseball interest carried no further. Nor did his presence muzzle the critics, one of whom patronized the game as "rounders played with . . . a bigger stick."[8] Except for the Japanese success, the third mission, like its predecessors, was a failure, although official baseball histories argue otherwise.

The obvious failure of the three formal baseball missions hardly dampened the missionary zeal of nationalistic baseball officials, who are accustomed to reaping where they have not sown. Far from admitting failure in their missionary activities, baseball officials still take credit for spreading the game to other lands. Over the years since 1920 small scale tours and spring training forays have shown major league ball to Latin America and Japan, where the game thrives lustily. The growing popularity of the game in such areas has kept alive the mission of America myth among baseball leaders in America. In 1966, for example, baseball Commissioner William D. (Spike) Eckert, an ex-Air Force general, declared baseball to be a potent tool of American foreign policy, and appointed the ebullient Roberto Maduro, an exiled Cuban and former baseball club owner there, to be coordinator of inter-American baseball. In a brash new version of the missionary myth, Maduro called on the United States State Department to purchase equipment to be donated to Latin American countries for the purpose of currying good will.

To Maduro, baseball is the antidote to anti-Yankee feelings: "Wherever baseball is played, there is pro-United States sentiment. Put a glove and ball and bat in the hands of a Latin American, and it makes him think indirectly of the United States and Democracy." Continuing this simplistic line, Maduro argued that in Latin American countries where baseball is played, Americans are liked; "but in Bogota, where it is not played, there is more anti-Yankee feeling."[9] More recently, the late Eckert's successor, Commissioner Bowie Kuhn, spoke expansively of major league baseball taking on teams in Japan and Latin America, with Europe and other world areas to follow.[10]

In evaluating such grandiose claims, students of sports need to bring tough anthropological insights to bear. Most important is the question of what sport or sports do most civilized peoples of the world prefer? The answer—probably soccer, or football as it is called. True, transplanted baseball has grown sturdily and popularly in Japan and Latin America, but the game as played and promoted in other lands carries the unique cultural markings of the peoples who play it. According to anthropologist Homer Barnett, any "configuration," which would include a game like baseball, "has a multiplicity of characteristics and hence a great number of potentials for combination." When placed in a different cultural setting and blended with different customs, a new version of baseball is created.[11] Some striking examples of differing species of baseball are found among peoples living outside the orbit of Western civilization. Thus, anthropologist John Honigmann has found an Eskimo variety of baseball that downplays individual competitiveness, and J. R. Fox, observing the game as played among the Cochitl Village Pueblo Indians, found the game functioning to displace sorcery by providing another means for repressing hostilities.[12]

As a cultural export, the acceptance or rejection of baseball by another society requires some sort of "advocate" to help the game take hold. As part of a general explanation of cultural change, Homer Barnett's analysis of advocacy is useful to the problem of understanding baseball's chances of making an impression on other cultures. According to Barnett, advocates champion change in culture. Among Barnett's classes of advocates are *professional advocates*, illustrated by the major league baseball missionaries, their agents, collaborators, and converts within a country. Another type, the *conservative advocate*, is illustrated by American colonists, administrators, businessmen and clergy, who, while dwelling in a foreign land, continue to play baseball, thus inspiring native imitators. A third class, *elite advocates*, is illustrated by upper class citizens of a country who, by embracing baseball themselves, inspire their followers to do likewise. And a final type, the *out-group advocate*, is illustrated by American soldiers who are accepted as allies or occupiers and whose baseball play inspires imitation. This has happened in areas where NATO forces are based.[13]

Viewed in this perspective, the spread of baseball took place by each of these forms of advocacy, sometimes singly, more often by combinations of types of advocacy. But the three great baseball missions were all undertaken under the mistaken notion that baseball could best be spread by professional advocacy, in the form of a spectacular display of the game as played by skilled professionals. While by no means a total failure, the results of these displays were disappointing and sometimes even counterproductive.

Certainly the attempts to convert Britain to baseball by professional advocacy were counterproductive. This was Henry Needham's contention in his criticism of the 1914 mission: "It was unfortunate, I think, that the idea was ever suggested of trying to . . . plant baseball on English turf. Especially unfortunate was the erroneous impression created that the purpose of our visit was to drive out cricket with baseball." Needham found British sportsmen put off by what they thought to be American chauvinism in baseball promotion. And they also were affronted by American competitiveness in sport: "The American idea . . . is to take any good game, become adept at it, and then, out of pure deviltry, beat the man who invented that game." [14]

Moreover, the very polish of the American professionals hurt the spread of baseball in Britain. This was the opinion of Frederic R. Sears, the American-born president of the British Baseball Association. In a verbose 1909 essay entitled "Baseball in Britain," he cited the impossibility of grasping the essentials of baseball in a single viewing of professionals at play. Bewildered by what they saw and affronted by the propaganda that accompanied the American visit, many Britishers were turned off. To Sears, the job of establishing baseball in Britain would require carefully planned movements, led by men like himself, who would draw on resources of organized American baseball for help, including perhaps the loan of professional players to beef up British teams.

But even with such aid Sears doubted baseball's ability to compete with British football. He noted that it was the practice of British football clubs to permit baseball teams to use their grounds, sometimes even allowing them to play exhibitions before the start of football matches. Although this gave succor and exposure to baseball, it stunted the growth of the game by presenting the game in shabby Cinderella fashion. Moreover, football promoters have been reluctant to share gate receipts with their baseball tenants.[15]

In other parts of Europe the outgroup advocacy of baseball by American troops has kindled a spark of interest in the game in such lands as Germany, the Netherlands, France, Italy, and Norway. In France local interest stimulated by American troop games prompted the Spalding company to print and sell a baseball primer written in French.[16] The same type of advocacy led an Italian to write a baseball primer in his own language. And NATO forces in Norway have inspired imitators in that land by their baseball play.[17]

Meanwhile Spain provides an interesting anthropological case in which baseball came to Spain via Cuba and was sustained by elite advocates. Baseball in Spain came via Cuban-born Spaniards who brought the game to Catalonia by 1924. There elite advocates played the game, using it as a vehicle for class distinction. Later four teams were formed, staffed mostly by elite gentlemen like Count Ramon of the Royal

Spanish Base Ball Club of Barcelona. But such elitist snobbery produced growing problems of a unique sort as the Catalonian League's first division came to regard the second division as contemptible social climbers. To gain prestige through victories teams of both divisions in that league recruited Americans as "ringers," passing them off as Basques or as Spanish-Americans. Nevertheless, Robert Boyle counted as many as 25,000 fans in attendance at games.[18]

But in countries like Canada, Japan, Mexico, and in Latin America baseball took root and grew hardily. In each of these areas baseball combined with native cultural practices to produce a new species of the game.[19] And by interacting with the American brand the feedback forced structural changes in American baseball. Canada is an obvious example. The recent entry of the Montreal Expos into the National League was an unprecedented structural change which made the major leagues truly international. Meanwhile Latin American participation in American minor professional leagues has influenced American baseball; most visibly by the presence of so many Latin American stars on major league rosters.[20] And a most memorable example of the American major leagues' reacting to outside baseball organization came in the late 1940s when a Mexican League official bought American stars in hopes of making the Mexican League a third major league. Although Jorge Pasquel's effort failed, Mexican baseball reaped a harvest of publicity and at this moment Mexico is considered a fertile ground for big league play.[21]

Elsewhere in Latin America the game shows dynamic growth. In Cuba young men who had attended American colleges introduced the game as early as 1865. As elite advocates in Cuba, they formed clubs and leagues. Further growth was stimulated by American soldiers occupying Cuba after the Spanish-American War. And later professional advocacy by American big league teams, like the Cincinnati Reds, Brooklyn Dodgers, and New York Giants, training in Cuba provided another growth stimulus. Thus Cubans had professional baseball teams of their own as early as 1901 and Cuban teams have played in American minor leagues. And if the Castro revolution ended such minglings, Castro's personal elite advocacy of baseball has contributed to the game's growth and development as a unique species of baseball.

With Cuba in the lead, other Latin Americans took to baseball. A measure of Latin American interest in baseball is seen in the game's presence in isolated rural areas. In the Dominican Republic politicos tried to ban the game as a corrupting Yankee or Cuban influence, but zealots like young Felipe Alou continued to play, using his hand as a bat and a lemon as a ball. Later Alou's father improvised better equipment, but Felipe was twelve years old before seeing a real ball.[22] Indeed, today Americans are dependent on Latin Americans for baseballs. In a Haitian plant workers, toiling at a dollar a day, turn out 3.7 million baseballs annually for export to the United States, where baseball sewing is said to be a nonexistent art.

That baseball is solidly entrenched in Latin America is evidenced in the competition in the Caribbean championship games. Now a quarter of a century old, these contests evoke nationalistic fervor. And in the Pan American games Cuban teams have defeated American amateurs several times.

But it is Japan that bids fair to become the baseball capital of the world. In no other land was American baseball so zealously accepted, or so effectively developed as a sports spectacular. Soon after the Meiji Reform era was under way, instituting as national policy controlled Westernization, American baseball took root. In 1873 an American teacher and baseball player introduced the game. Soon after this, native elite advocates at the university of Keio and Waseda introduced the game and generations of students became baseball players. By 1896 teams from these universities defeated a visiting American team, and by 1913 Japanese teams defeated Filipinos at the Far Eastern Olympics.[23]

When the 1914 American baseball mission arrived, they met an enthusiastic reception. Although the American professionals defeated local teams, Manager McGraw of the Giants foresaw a different story in the future: "These little brown fellows have the makings of good performers. They are fast and think well, always being in the game and taking chances. Once they caught as smart a ballplayer as Speaker napping off second base in as pretty a double play as you could see in the big league." [24]

From 1914 on Japan aimed at matching American standards of play. Less publicized tours of American professional teams, as organized by Frank O'Doul in 1931 and 1934, were equally impressed by Japanese baseball virtuosity. By then Japan was a "baseball crazy" nation, and games of the newly formed Professional Baseball League of Japan were publicized by press and radio. In 1939 this league drew 620,000 fans for the season and the Tokyo team had a park with a seating capacity of 60,000. [25]

During the war the Japanese military government banned professional baseball and sought to rid the amateur game of Americanisms. But with the war's end, professional baseball returned to heightened popularity. In 1947 it outdrew Sumo wrestling, which had been the militarists' choice for Japan's national sport. In the early postwar years Sotaro Suzuki, vice-president of the Nippon Professional Baseball League, coined the slogan, "Follow American Ball," which struck a responsive chord. Outfield fences were shortened to allow for more home runs, American baseball jargon was introduced, and American customs like having dignitaries toss out the first ball and the custom of bickering with umpires came in. [26] American major league teams were welcomed and discarded American major leaguers were signed to play on Japanese teams. Of course such Americanisms did not prevent the unique development of Japanese baseball, which differed in crowd behavior, control of the game, and style of play. So far Japanese professionals seem content to play at home and to vie in their own World Series. But increasingly there are talks of merging American and Japanese major leagues. However, it seems that any merger of international baseball interests must be negotiated among equals. Today Japan has its own superstars, franchises and traditions. Indeed, given the fact of greater popularity of the game both in Japan and Latin America, might not control over an international baseball association pass out of American hands, as in the recent case of auto production? To the internationalist-minded this might be a godsend, but how does this grab an American chauvinist?

While awaiting the future realization of an international baseball concordat, one daily observes the towering presence of so many Latin-American stars in major league uniforms. In the brilliant play of the late Roberto Clemente, or Manny Sanguillen, Luis Tiant, Juan Marichal, and others, what lessons are to be learned? If such men were to join together in major league teams from their own lands, could Americans hope to best them? And what if black Americans were to group into teams of their own; how then would white Americans fare? Obviously these are divisive questions, but they prod the serious student of sport to question prevailing myths like the one that assumes the superiority of American culture. Now may well be the time for baseball officials to lay aside the mission of America myth in favor of realistic cosmopolitan understanding.

NOTES

1. Ralph H. Gabriel, *The Course of American Democratic Thought: An Intellectual History Since 1815* (New York: Ronald Press, 1941); Frederick Merk, *Manifest Destiny in American History: A Reinterpretation* (New York: Knopf, 1962), pp. 3–4, 261–66.

2. David Quentin Voigt, *Cash and Glory: The Commercialization of Major League Baseball as a Sports Spectacular* (Syracuse University Ph.D. thesis, 1962), pp. 126–32. Also Harry Clay Palmer, *Athletic Sports in America, England, and Australia* (Philadelphia; Hubbard Bros., 1889), pp. 88–89.

3. (Chicago: A. G. Spalding and Bros., 1888). Palmer, *Athletic Sports,* pp. 151–460.

4. *Sporting News,* Feb. 9, 1889; April 18, 1891. *Sporting Life,* Feb. 20, 27, 1889.

5. *Spalding's Official Baseball Guide. 1890.*

6. *Spalding Guide, 1910,* pp. 299–305.

7. T. P. Sullivan, *History of World's Tour—Chicago White Sox and New York Giants* (Chicago: M. Donahue Co., 1914). Ring Lardner, *The Homecoming of John McGraw, Charles Comiskey, and James J. Callahan* (Souvenir booklet, 1914). "Australian Idea of Baseball," *Literary Digest,* Feb. 21, 1914.

8. Henry B. Needham, "Baseball and the Briton," *Colliers,* April 4, 1914.

9. *New York Times,* June 5, 1966. *Sporting News,* Feb. 18, 1967.

10. *New York Times,* Nov. 22, 1967; July 23, 1969.

11. Homer Barnett, *Innovation: The Basis of Cultural Change* (New York: McGraw-Hill, 1953), p. 186.

12. For a summation of these and other studies see David Q. Voigt, *America's Leisure Revolution: Essays in the Sociology of Leisure and Sports* (Reading, Pa.: Albright College Printing Office, 1971), pp. 65–67.

13. Barnett, *Innovation,* pp. 291–311.

14. Needham, "Baseball and the Briton."

15. Frederic R. Sears, "Baseball in Britain," *Spalding Guide* (British ed.,), 1909. See also *Records of Fulwood Amateur Baseball Club,* London, England; New York Public Library, microfilm.

16. J. B. Foster, *Comment on Joue A La Alle Au Camp* (New York: American Sports, 1919).

17. Alberto Manetta, *Il Baseball* (Roma: Edzioni Mediterranee, 1960).

18. Robert H. Boyle, "Baseball in Spain," *Atlantic,* Oct. 1954, pp. 110–11.

19. Collie Small, "Baseball's Improbable Imports," *Saturday Evening Post,* Aug. 2, 1952.

20. *Spalding Guide* (Spanish-American ed.), *1910,* pp. 23 ff. George C. Compton and Adolfo Diaz, "Latins on the Diamond," *Americas,* June 1951, pp. 9–11, 40.

21. Milton Bracker, "Beisbol 'Hits' a 'Jonron' Down Mexico Way," *New York Times Magazine,* June 9, 1946.

22. Felipe Alou with Herman Weiskopf, *Felipe Alou—My Life in Baseball* (Waco, Texas: Word Books, 1967), pp. 12–17.

23. B. W. Fleischer, "Baseball in Japan," *Colliers,* Jan. 2, 1909, p. 29.

24. "An Oriental Olympic," *Colliers,* May 1913. "Baseball in Japan," *Outlook,* Jan. 1914. Robert Trumbull, "Japan: Baseball Fever," *Holiday,* Oct. 1961.

25. "Baseball-Crazy Japs," *Current History,* September 1940, p. 52.

26. Norman Cousins, "Slide, Fujimura, Slide," *Colliers,* Aug. 2, 1947. Weldon James, "Japan's at Batto Again," *Colliers,* Aug. 2, 1947.

8

American baseball and the American dilemma

High on the list of divisive social problems threatening the American nation is the rift between black and
white Americans. Although America's racist confrontation is
but a single front of a great global confrontation between
white and colored peoples, our front of battle is the most visible, the most scrutinized, and the most publicized. This
dubious record is a product of centuries of racist oppression,
each generation contributing its links to a chainlike problem
that today so ensnares as to baffle disengagement.

The trouble began with the American slave system, the
most oppressive and inhuman of the several modern forms of
slavery.[1] An end to the system had much of the apocalyptic
drama of an Old Testament prophecy come true as war, con-
fiscation, occupation, and fiatistic magic were combined to
"end" the system. That it did not end, but merely shaded
into another form of oppression—systematic discrimination
with all the hurt, guilt, and hypocrisy accompanying—explains the phenomenom that Swedish sociologist Gunnar
Myrdal called the American dilemma.

The American dilemma had its immediate origins in the Union victory of 1865, a triumph viewed then as a righteous Armageddon. In the wake of victory, three amendments to the Constitution promised full equality for black people, while Congressional reconstruction programs tried to prepare blacks and Southerners for integrated democracy. This era of lofty hopes lasted from 1865 to 1877 and was dashed by the shabby political compromise of 1876. With the failure came the American dilemma. Roughly defined, the American dilemma is a shattered ideal, an admission that we as a nation committed to freedom are not capable of living up to our promise that such freedom shall be for all Americans. Thus, the dilemma is the mirror of our hypocrisy, and the reflection we see undermines our faith in our ability to live democratically. If over the years we have learned to live with the dilemma and to rationalize in various ways our shortcomings, Myrdal thought that our denial of freedom and equality to blacks was a blotch on our national character.[2]

As for black Americans, after a brief decade of spurious freedom they were obliged to live lives of imposed social restriction, separating them from white members of society. The segregated life required them to accept the myth of the polluting power of blackness; a submission which required blacks to limit their associations in such matters as residence, marriage, worship, school, and play to the company of other blacks. A complex web of lifeways, segregation was imposed and implemented by a maze of customs and laws known as Jim Crow laws. Sanctified by religious, biological, and social myths, the code by 1900 operated in all regions of America, with the South spinning the most elaborate net because most blacks then lived in that region. However, as more blacks migrated to the industrial cities of the North and West, they were ghettoed in slums that were recently abandoned by hyphenated American minorities who were moving toward fuller participation in American society. But if white minorities could feed on the myth of higher status as the fruit of hard work, this myth held little promise for black Americans. They

107

were the pariahs, the "unmeltable Americans" whose presence in society was a nasty reminder of the inconsistencies of American democracy. Perhaps the main function of segregation was to make blacks "invisible," so as to assuage the guilt feelings engendered by daily confrontation.[3]

The policy of enforced segregation lasted for two generations after 1900. But by 1940 the social costs of maintaining a dual society were becoming unbearable. That more than 10 million Americans should remain servile, undereducated, and economically unproductive, adversely affected both the peacetime economy of 1940 and later the wartime economy. Federal policies barring discrimination came out of our wartime consensus and Supreme Court decisions striking down discrimination in key institutions turned the tide by the mid-1950s. Today the prospect of integrating 20 million black Americans into complete and equal participation in major areas of life still remains a doubtful option. But with more black Americans better schooled in techniques of wielding power, many are opting for some form of separatism, at least the control over key institutions like businesses and schools, as a more acceptable solution to their plight than a spurious ethic of integration.

"Benign neglect" was the descriptive term coined by Nixonian politics for the ongoing drama of American racist relations. Ours is a period of deceptive calm, but many are aware of the divisive threat to the American nation posed in this confrontation. To save the Union is still the great challenge, and if met, it will be because rising expectations of black equality have been met. But even to palliate ills of the past requires a knowledge of symptoms, and to gain such knowledge requires thorough study of today's racial scene in the light of the sordid history of black and white relations. To tell the story as it was means relating the effects of exclusionary practices in each of our institutions, especailly those which have prided themselves on being relatively innocent.

MAJOR LEAGUE BASEBALL'S EQUALITARIAN CLAIMS

American sports in general, and professional baseball in particular, have accepted unearned credit for being repositories of democratic energy. In major league baseball the myth of equality holds that the "national game" always afforded opportunities for hard-working, talented youths. Because a player is judged on performance, the myth of equality in baseball proclaims that American boys consistently surmounted lowly origins to reap cash and glory in the major leagues. As evidence, baseball historians point to patterns of invasion and succession by various immigrant groups, patterns that mirror American immigration history. Thus, Irish-Americans rose to stardom by the 1880s, followed by German-Americans, Italian-Americans, Polish-Americans, and presently black-Americans and Latin-Americans. Nor was religion a barrier, as evidenced by a repeated sprinkling of Jewish stars over the past century—including Lipman Pike, Andy Cohen, Harry Danning, Hank Greenberg, Sid Gordon, Sandy Koufax, and Ron Blomberg. Thus was the myth of baseball's democratic purity spun out. With it went the moral suggesting that if only other social institutions could be as equalitarian as baseball, America's dilemma would be less a problem.

Like all myths this one contains an element of truth. But falsities abound, and the historical evidence mocks baseball's claim to being a lighthouse guiding the way to full social equality for all Americans. Indeed, to undertake the demythologizing of official baseball history on this point is to learn anew the blunt fact that sports seldom shape cultural change, but usually lag behind by reflecting the prevailing customs and values of an era.

The early history of major league baseball reflects the unfolding ethical dilemma of a nation which freed its slaves, but could not bring itself to grant equality to the freedmen. What to do with the blacks was the question of the era, and honest answers were confounded by ideological clashings. On the one horn of the dilemma was the rhetoric of freedom, sanctified by the war's outcome and by the martyred Lincoln. On the other horn was the deeply rooted notion that blacks were subhuman, unclean, and unfit for social equality. As the nation groped for an equilibrium, it gradually became evident that blacks could be barred from white institutions without degrading the idea of equality. But if such mendacity required agility in compartmentalizing opposing values, most Americans proved equal to the test. In the end the blacks suffered the great psychological anguish of being obliged to accept the notion of freedom while realistically adjusting to a life of imposed inequality.

American baseball vividly mirrors the unfolding pattern of a segregationist solution to the American dilemma. In the 1880s two educated black players from Ohio, Moses Fleetwood Walker and his brother Welday, sought major league careers. In 1884 both signed with Toledo in the American Association (then a major league), where Fleet, who batted .251 in forty-one games, showed promise as a catcher. Welday, batting .182 in six games as an outfielder, hardly had a chance. But that year the color bar clanged down on both brothers and neither got a chance to further prove himself.

Later Welday Walker accused Adrian Anson, captain and superstar of the Chicago White Stockings, of leading the opposition against all colored players. Anson was charged with employing "all the venom . . . of a Tillman or a Vardaman" to bar Manager John Ward of the Giants from playing Negro pitcher, George Stovey. This Anson freely admitted; in his autobiography he takes credit out of his own personal dislike of all blacks! Today it seems incredible that one man's hatred could influence policy. That Anson succeeded illustrates how wide the value gap is between our era and that of the 1880s. Ours is an age of legal domination which requires anyone who would influence legislation to marshal facts and prove his position.

In Anson's era facts about blacks were damning. At best, baseball fans regarded black players as curiosities; at worst, they badgered them with insults. Such was the case of Vincent Nava, a catcher with the Providence Grays of the National League from 1882–84, and with Baltimore of the American Association until 1886. Nava, whose real name was Irwin Sandy, was variously "passed" as a Spaniard, Mexican, and Italian, but his dark skin repeatedly branded him as a Negro. Racist taunts made Nava's baseball life a nightmare. Similar treatment drove out another would-be "passer," George Treadway, a hard-hitting outfielder for the National League Baltimore Orioles in the 1890s. Attempts were made to pass Treadway as an Indian, but a tide of hostility drove him out after 1896, despite his lifetime .292 batting average.

Treadway's case ended the tactic of trying to pass colored players as members of other minorities. In 1901 Manager John McGraw tried to pass black pitcher Charles Grant, but when Grant was seen in the company of some black friends a wave of protest forced American League officials to nullify his contract.

The acquiescence of baseball officials in the Grant case reflects American solidarity behind segregation practices. At the turn of the century, baseball in company with railroads, hotels, restaurants, and other public institutions was segregated by customs and laws. In baseball, an elaborate code of customary law accomplished the deed. Major league club-owners acting in concert promulgated a segregationist code that barred blacks from "organized baseball." [4]

Baseball's segregation policies reflected widespreading exclusionary practices throughout the land. Supported by social Darwinian ideologies, blacks were harried from white teams and forced to form their own black leagues, such as the Negro National League. But such separatism only strengthened segregation and worsened the lot of black players. According to Sol White's guide, by 1900 the best stars of the Negro leagues averaged $466 a year, considerably below the $571 average for white *minor* leaguers and far below the $2,000 average for white major leaguers.

Along with low pay went a loss of human dignity. In Walker's embittered account, one reads of Negro players denied hotel accommodations and forced to walk the streets at night. And because there was money to be made in playing exhibition games with white teams, Negro teams often endured the bitter humiliations of such games for the money. At such contests the segregation code allowed white players and fans to deride blacks without retaliation. All joined in the humiliation game, including sportswriters like Tim Murnane, sports editor of the *Boston Globe*, who once wrote: "There is an array of colored players around the large cities. Their playing is more picturesque to look at than their pale-faced brothers." At this time white managers like Ted Sullivan delighted in goading black teams at exhibitions, using devices like holding the score to 11–7 (a "craps score"), and breaking watermelons in front of the black team's dugout.[6]

THE COLOR BAR IN AMERICAN BASEBALL

For half a century after 1900, except for occasional exhibition games played between white and black teams, the color segregation of major league baseball was complete. In defense of the policy, proponents used the separate but equal argument, but in reality Negro baseball, like segregation in schooling and housing, doomed blacks to social inferiority. Plagued by inadequate financing, the Negro major leagues suffered from organizational difficulties, shaky franchises, poor playing facilities, scanty publicity, and wretched accommodations for players and fans.[7] In retrospect, the invisibility of Negro baseball is the most remarkable fact. The *Sporting News*, long the self-proclaimed bible of American baseball, pursued a conspiracy of silence toward Negro baseball. Thus, scores, standings, and records of play went unreported.[8]

In the Jim Crow era, when a black baseball hopeful like

LeRoy "Satchel" Paige sought a career in baseball, he joined a Negro minor league team. In Satch's case he got his expense money and a share of a keg of lemonade at the end of each game. This was in 1924, and Satch recalled a white scout watching him pitch, saying, "We sure could use you. If only you was white." An oft-repeated refrain, Paige heard it over the next twenty years, and it ever reminded him of the polluting power of his blackness—a stigma so strong as to override his brilliant 30–1 pitching record of 1924, his skein of twenty-six consecutive pitching victories in 1926, and all the glowing achievements he accomplished in Negro baseball up to 1948. Among his most prized achievements were his successes against white major leaguers in exhibition games. Once, in 1930, he struck out twenty-two white major leaguers in a game, including Sam Agnew, who once caught Walter Johnson and thought Paige to be faster than the Senator star. And if Babe Ruth refused to bat against Paige, other stars, like Babe Herman, Hack Wilson, and Joe Di Maggio did, and came away marveling at Paige's speed and control.

As a superstar of black baseball Paige earned up to $22,000 a year by playing summers in Negro major leagues, and barnstorming and playing winter baseball. Altogether he pitched an estimated 2,500 games, including 153 games in a single year.

His fame was such that whites often came to black parks to see him pitch. Yet it could not be the other way around. In the 1930s, Paige's team was barred from using League Park, home of the Cleveland Indians. Naturally Paige felt himself exploited by the white establishment. And sometimes Latin-Americans did the same. In 1937 President Trujillo of the Dominican Republic offered Paige several thousand dollars to pitch in Ciudad Trujillo, but Paige soon discovered that Trujillo only wanted help in humbling a political rival who happened to be a baseball promoter. Yet, on the whole, Latin-American countries afforded a respite from American discrimination. A perennial barnstormer, Paige recalled having to eat in a backroom standing up and being told by hotel clerks that "We don't serve niggers," among other outrages.

Moreover, even when he was called up to the Cleveland Indians in the twilight of his career, insults continued.[9]

Paige shone brightest among a galaxy of colored stars whose performances with black teams are celebrated now in a newly created National Black Sports Hall of Fame.[10] Among the earlier stars was Frank Grant of Buffalo in the Negro International League, who once caught a foul fly by climbing eight feet up a telephone pole. So remarkable was Grant's play that he often was compared to the great Ed Delahanty, star of the Philadelphia Phillies. Yet Grant was no exception, for at every point in the Jim Crow era, black players matched the prowesses of white major leaguers.[11] Belatedly this fact is now recognized in the admission of several black stars to the Baseball Hall of Fame at Cooperstown. However, this shrine affords Paige and others a special niche—an ironic symbol of the grudging ground given to the fading of discrimination in America.

Until the end of World War II white baseball leaders stood solidly against blacks' invading the majors, except perhaps in the role of clown or scapegoat, like "Smokey," who was John McGraw's trainer and the butt of so many cruel jokes.[12] Moreover, the baseball establishment took the "white only" policy for granted. Marveling at the effectiveness of baseball's "unwritten law," Westbrook Pegler wrote in 1931 that in all his years as sports editor of the *Chicago Tribune*, he never once received a letter protesting the color bar in baseball. Protesting its lack of logic, Pegler wondered how the South allowed blacks to watch white games, but refused to allow blacks to play on white teams.[13] One might ask, where were the liberal opponents of bigotry, that one like Pegler, later the spokesman of America's paranoid right, should stand alone in protesting the situation? Certainly, few liberals took up the cause of baseball integration, although in 1938 the staff of the *Nation* led a protest against a radio station which allowed Jake Powell, a southern-born Yankee outfielder, to say on the air that his favorite hobby was "cracking niggers on the head" as a Dayton, Ohio, policeman. Such protests evoked an official denunciation of Powell's "uncouth chauvinism," [14] but continued exclusion of blacks passed without criticism. Later, a few less tremulous writers, like Jimmy Powers of the *New York Daily News* and Shirley Povich of the *Washington Post*, attacked the color bar. Such attacks, combined with wartime democratic rhetoric, moved President Frick of the National League to promise that soon blacks would play in the majors. [15]

Still the realization of such a promise depended on major league owners, who, if they had their way, would have kept blacks waiting till today. Determined to delay integration as long as possible, they gave ground only under strong pressure from outside institutions. Changes in black economic position provided the strongest counterweight against the owners' policy. Inspired by the New Deal, by the willingness of the CIO labor organization to admit Negroes, and by blacks' winning access to defense jobs in World War II, the principle of black equality in economic pursuits was gaining acceptance in America—or at least lip service. And with economic power went political clout. The end of the war found black power groups in a position to win political concessions in payment for the cooperation of these groups during the war. Indeed, the federal government now was committed to fostering equalitarian policies. [16] The commitment was backed by the pressures of black migration to northern cities, where black political power was now felt. Meanwhile the culminating effects of a knowledge explosion which blasted myths of Negro inferiority, ineptitude and animality, helped push the drive for equality, as did a boom in college attendance which exposed many to new facts on the meaning and morality of race.

BASEBALL AND THE INTEGRATION ETHIC

As increased money, political clout, and knowledge empowered blacks, white baseball owners became more interested in tapping the increasing purchasing power of blacks. Although personally committed to integration, Bill Veeck,

Jr., in 1943 a hustling, young promoter out to win fame and fortune as a big league club owner, admitted as much. That year he tried to buy the moribund Phillies franchise, which he planned to turn into a contender by stocking the team with black stars like Paige. But at the time a coalition of major league owners barred the sale to Veeck, choosing instead, first a gambler, and then a DuPont executive.[17]

Two years later, in 1945, a baseball insider moved to carry out a similar strategy. That year, Branch Rickey, the respected and highly successful general manager who built the Cardinals into a champion dynasty and was about to do the same with the Dodgers, moved to test the unwritten law. As part owner of the Dodgers, general manager Rickey gauged the potential attendance power of black baseball fans in Brooklyn. Aside from profit, Rickey was partly motivated by altruism and by fear of black political clout. He suffered a blow from that clout when, in the spring of 1945, a group of civil libertarians tried to use New York State's Ives-Quinn antidiscrimination law against major league baseball. The move forced Rickey to give a tryout to two black players, and although both were rejected, the sponsors called the attempt a first step in lowering the color bar. Fearing similar power plays in the future, Rickey opted for gradual, voluntary, evolutionary integration, assuring the rejected pair that "I'm more for your cause than anybody else you know."[18]

Brave words those, but in retrospect they included the patronizing platitudes that made blacks so cynical toward the integration ethic. More in tune with black sentiments were these words spoken in reply to Rickey by the black sponsors: "We've been put off long enough."[19]

If Rickey's tepid liberalism represented the radical position among major league owners, the conservatism of most of the others matched that of extreme segregationists. As reported to a 1946 Congressional subcommittee looking into monopoly practices by major league owners, the owners defended their racist policy on three counts: 1) there were too few good black players, 2) the separate Negro major leagues would be hurt by integration, and, 3) outside agitators were conspiring to cripple major league baseball by branding it racist.[20] The logic of such arguments is mind boggling, especially the point that Negro major leagues can operate in spite of having only a few good players. And the third point is the old paranoid conspiracy theory, which in our time has been much over-used; most recently it was invoked to justify Watergate break-ins by Republican politicos.

Publically major league owners continued to use discred-ited Social Darwinian rhetoric to justify their stand. In 1945 President Leland S. MacPhail of the Yankees argued that Negroes must prove that they possess "ability, character, and aptitude" to play major league ball. MacPhail also used the old "black peril" myth, arguing that white fans would tol-erate only a limited number "of Negro players." And MacPhail also argued that Negro players lacked the coordi-nation and competitive spirit of white players.[21]

Most frequently employed was the stereotyped explanation that all members of a "race" exhibit the same behavior. Be-cause this fallacy of race is still commonly held, it fuels the psychological war between blacks and whites. William Kunstler, the noted civil rights attorney of our day, thought this fact to be expressed by the "simple feeling in the gut of every white man that he is superior to all black people."[22] Knowing whites hold this view deepens black hostilities.

Such myths live on. In major league baseball, as in other institutions, blacks still encounter the myth of the "black peril" and the myth that race determines behavior potential. Hence, by winning the right to play in the majors blacks overcame the color bar only to encounter hidden, psycho-logical barriers. Such is the context within which one must view present-day trends in baseball's accommodating of black players.

Given the continuing reality of psychological rejection, the popular legend of Jackie Robinson's triumph in becoming the first black player to make the majors has a phoney ring to it. As the legend goes, Rickey made good on his 1945 promise by signing Jack Roosevelt Robinson to a Dodger contract in 1946. An intelligent, college-educated war veteran, Robinson gratefully accepted the challenge, and took on his broad shoulders the task of "proving" that qualified blacks could hold their own in the majors. In succeeding Robinson supposedly confirmed the reality of the American dream—that blacks too, by dint of hard work and by exhibiting good, middle-class white behavior, could make the grade in any social institution. Moreover, Robinson's example supposedly proved the efficacy of the integration ethic as a way of solving our racial dilemma.

That many players and fans refused to accept the integration ethic was evidenced in the paranoid reactions to Robinson's presence on major league diamonds. From the beginning he was humiliated. White players berated him with epithets and some members of the Dodgers drew up a petition against him, while a cabal of Cardinals tried to block his debut in the majors by threatening a strike.[23] Although President Frick nipped the strike attempt by threatening to suspend all participants and by jointly announcing with American League President William Harridge and Commissioner A. B. Chandler support for Robinson, many baseball owners opposed Robinson's entry. In 1948, Rickey told a black student audience at Wilberforce State University that some owners had petitioned for a halt to further integration on the grounds of a "black peril" threat. Rickey's exposure of the report forced its withdrawal, but many owners remained stubbornly hostile.[24]

Certainly high level opposition cut deep. In 1946 President W. G. Bramham of the National Association of Professional Baseball Players (an organization of minor leagues) sneered at Rickey, saying, "We can expect Rickey Temple to be in the course of construction at Harlem soon." Even the Negro major leagues opposed the experiment until pressure from black newspapers forced them to reconsider. And in Florida, where in 1946 Robinson began training with the Montreal

Royals, Jim Crow opposition forced the Dodgers to move their entire training program to escape the pressure from local segregation customs.[25] Later, in playing at Montreal, fans at first expressed hostility, but they soon accepted Robinson and acclaimed his stout performance. But then, on joining the Dodgers in 1947 Robinson faced renewed hostility from fans and sometimes had his life threatened by cranks.

To his credit as a planner, Rickey had anticipated many of these reactions and his strategy was to teach Robinson how to cope with them. Such a strategy reflected the prevailing climate of race relations. It assumed that Robinson was shouldering the future of many would-be black players; hence, Robinson was obliged to "prove" himself worthy of white company, by abiding taunts and epithets, by keeping his temper at all times. Rickey even manipulated Robinson's love life by asking him if he had a girl and telling him if he did, to marry her immediately. Embedded in this prescription is a myth of super black sexuality, which leads whites to suspect that the black design aims at sexual integration of the races.

Stoically playing the role of "guinea pig," Robinson did all that Rickey asked and thereby paid a heavy psychological price. At the end of the 1946 season, after he had batted .349 and helped Montreal to a Little World Series victory, Robinson's hair turned gray and he came close to experiencing a nervous breakdown. But the following year he wore a Dodger uniform.

Viewed in retrospect, Rickey's strategy was the familiar "niggerization" formula tailored to Robinson. In donning Rickey's suggested "armor of humility," Robinson had to become "a white man's nigger." This meant patiently awaiting the pleasure of patronizing whites to accept him as a performer and human being. And Robinson waited. Cast in the role of "loner," he roomed, ate, and relaxed alone, all the time affecting a quiet and unassuming personality. In time the grueling ordeal of resocialization eased, and he came to be accepted for his fine play. By consistent hitting and fielding he became a star and later was able to doff his docile personality and take on his own naturally combative and competitive character.[26]

But in doffing the role, Robinson paid further dues. For venting his temper on his attackers, he was pegged by the new Dodger owners as a troublemaker. Thus, the close of his ten-year career with the Dodgers left him alienated from baseball. For him there were no offers to coach or to manage, so Robinson struck back by announcing his retirement in an exclusive *Look* magazine article published in 1957. A final gesture of defiance, it widened the rift between himself and the Dodger owner.

Yet by initially playing the role of "white man's nigger," Robinson undoubtedly speeded the admission of more blacks. For this Robinson has been honored by baseball mythmakers as the brave pioneer who integrated baseball. Today, some twenty years later, the legend is fixed in baseball folklore, boosted over the years by its retelling in articles, books, movies, and by Robinson's election to Baseball's Hall of Fame.[27]

While fully aware of the phoniness of the legend, Robinson manipulated it in the cause of racial justice. The legend also served his postbaseball business career, which by the time of his death in 1972 ranked him among the foremost of America's black businessmen. With a personal worth of $200,000 Robinson used his post as director of the Hamilton Life Insurance Company to advance the cause of black capitalism by increasing the number of black agencies. As a businessman, Robinson's moderate approach to the racial question stressed business success and political clout as superior to revolution. Dynamic and flexible, he swung with the changing winds of black rhetoric. This led him to break with the Republican party over the nominations of Goldwater and Nixon, both of whom he labeled racist. But always he held up the example of his personal success as a guideline to young blacks. Perhaps, because he was born out of time, he saw merit in both the integrationist and black power positions. As he said once, "We didn't see other problems. But the kids today are taking a better look because in many places you'd be in trouble if you didn't get involved."[28] Toward the end of his life he was often ridiculed by black power extremists, and his personal life was blighted by the tragic death of an elder son. The bittersweet overtones of Robinson's career are admirably played out by Roger Kahn in his book *The Boys of Summer*.[29]

Had he remained in baseball, Robinson might have weighed the hopelessness of the integration ethic. Based on belief in the good faith of whites which was too often misplaced, it might have persuaded him to destroy his own legend. Toward the end of his life he spoke bitterly to Milton Richmond: "I think it's a tragedy that baseball is still wallowing in the nineteenth century saying Negroes can't manage white ballplayers." Noting the owners' stubborn refusal to yield on this point, Robinson was glad he was off the scene: "Had I remained ... my life would have been in the same narrow strata that baseball people are in today."[30]

Beset by paranoid fear, some white owners substituted subtler forms of discrimination for the discredited color bar. In 1957, the year Robinson retired, Rickey admitted that a quota system existed in the majors. Earlier, when still the Dodgers' general manager, he recalled that five of his directors had said that the Dodgers had too many blacks on the team.[31] And if the year 1959 saw fifty black men in the majors, sportswriters generally conceded that these men were better than a random sampling of the same number of white players. As a sociological study of the late 1960s showed, black pitchers were consistently better than white ones, and black batters generally hit for higher averages than whites. The study suggested that blacks cannot make the majors as ordinary performers although whites can and do. As proof, performance records of 1967 were used to show that twenty-three National League blacks and seventeen American League blacks accounted for over half of the base hits made in the majors that year. Moreover, black players got less cash for their performances and were more promptly discarded when their effectiveness declined. Also lacking is glory, since the most lavish publicity and opportunities for endorsements went to whites.[32] The year of 1973 showed a glaring example of the truth of this point. That year as the thirty-nine-year-old Henry Aaron closed in on Babe Ruth's record of 714 lifetime homers, publicity mills whipped up none of the excitement that had accompanied the efforts of white performers such as Roger Maris, Denny McLain, or Steve Carlton. Worse, Aaron received considerable hate mail and was often verbally assaulted by Atlanta fans.[33]

Until quite recently no black player was employed as a major league coach. In 1969 Elston Howard of the Yankees held a coaching position, but not until 1974 did a black man become a manager. In that year Frank Robinson was named to manage the 1975 Cleveland Indians.[34] Also, if Emmett Ashford, a college educated showman, who battled blacks as well as whites while on duty, served as a major league umpire, he waited long to get there. Fifty-one years old when he signed with the American League, he was frequently taunted with racist epithets. After five years, he retired in 1970 with a $1,600 annual pension.[35]

To blacks American baseball must resemble a problem for blacks to solve, rather than the other way around. Consider the frustrating pangs of rejection when black stars find white fans refusing to identify with them. As Sam Smith, president of the Southern League once put it: "Let's face it, there are folks down here who just don't want their kids growing up to admire a Negro ballplayer even if he's Willie Mays or Hank Aaron." The same kind of psychological rejection affects major league fans.[36] For example, Bob Gibson, star pitcher of the Cardinals, stated that a black major leaguer faces hundreds of subtle indignities: "When I was younger, things didn't aggravate me as much. When you get older . . . it makes you angry. It's almost like being punched in the nose all the time . . . you flinch." Gibson had come to see the day of equality for all major league players as far off: "The All-American boy isn't black. He's crewcut and he's blond. . . ."[37]

Fearful, perhaps, of fan reactions to the "black peril," owners have turned to Latin America in their talent searchings. By the late 1950s a white talent scarcity led owners to center talent hunts in Latin America, including Puerto Rico, the Virgin Islands, and the independent nations of Cuba, Panama, Mexico, and the Dominican Republic. Thus, by 1965 more than seventy Latin-American players wore major league uniforms. But like blacks, Latin-American players encountered psychological discrimination and suffered the same racial slights, as fans and writers tried hard to assign traditional color categories to them.[38] And little help was given Latin-Americans to cushion their cultural shock; not until 1971 did a major league club hit upon the idea of offering free English classes to them.[39]

With Latin-Americans and blacks facing similar problems, one wonders if in 1947, had black leaders been able to peer into the future, they would have acquiesced in the destruction of the all-black major leagues. In the light of today's continuance of racial separation, such leagues, competing against the white majors, might have gone far toward validating the claim that black is beautiful. With white American boys showing less interest in baseball, there is every chance that a black major league could have eclipsed the white majors.

Of course, this is speculation. The present pattern of artistic domination by black players reflects the agonies of a split society trying to restructure its institutions on the basis of equality. Complicating the difficulty is the choice of a path—shall it be an integrated or a separated path? Meanwhile racial tensions have exploded in urban rioting and unrest, and if such overt conflicts have lately quieted, American baseball mirrors the sullen feelings over the unresolved issues that triggered them. In the urban rioting which made the phrase "long hot summer" a frightening one in the late 1960s, major league baseball franchises located in troubled areas suffered financially. Especially the American League Chicago White Sox, whose park is located on the south side of that city in a racially troubled area, suffered. In 1968 tensions helped to cut attendance to an average of only 7,000 over a sixty-three-game stretch, prompting owners to consider moving the franchise. Elsewhere clubs abandoned old urban quarters, so that it is not farfetched to say that the franchise shifts of the 1960s and today are in large measure an example of baseball mirroring the middle-class white flights to the suburbs.[40]

In 1968 the fires of racial unrest were fed by the assassination of Martin Luther King, Jr., the great advocate of nonviolent integration. His death, coming at the beginning of the baseball campaign, moved black players to demand that scheduled games be canceled out of respect. When teams like the Dodgers responded slowly, racial tensions increased, as Jackie Robinson excoriated Dodger owner Walter O'Malley for his "total lack of knowledge of the frustrations of the Negro community." [41]

Smouldering bitterness still characterizes relations between black and white players, and sometimes white fans stir sparks. In 1968 Bob Gibson told a reporter about the hate mail he received. In a four-day period that year he received a hundred letters, including one urging him and "other blackbirds" to take their low mentalities back to Africa; others, attacking his sullen manner; another, his lack of cooperation; and others, his dandy and effeminate style of dress. Later, after his incredible, record-breaking feat of striking out seventeen Tigers in the first game of the 1968 World Series, a letter-writer rapped him for daring to break the record held by white pitcher Sandy Koufax. This parallels 1973 criticisms of Hank Aaron for daring to assault Ruth's record. Small wonder that Gibson felt "surly and bitter" about the disrespect shown black stars.[42]

In search of respect, along with cash and glory, baseball stars like Bill White and Maury Wills have joined the sports committee of the NAACP. But there are other ways of participating in "the movement." Today the civil rights movement resembles a flow of lava down the sides of an active volcano; only its general direction of flow is clear, for there are always varying eddies, stops, and starts. So it is with "the movement." Some groups favor black athletic rebellion, and they are encouraged by Harry Edwards, a black professor of sociology. Others prefer the individualism of a Jim Brown or Bill Russell. Most seem to be learning that sports is no royal road to equality. Today, the black who overemphasizes sports as the way to equality is apt to be criticized for prostituting himself to whites; for letting himself be ogled as an animal in a zoo. In Edwards' words, "The black athlete was the institutionalized Tom, the white man's nigger." Edwards urges all black athletes to commit themselves to "the cause" or be branded "house niggers."

Men like Edwards are exposing the subtle trap that ensnares black athletes in sports. Marshaling statistics, he has shown that black baseball players are mostly consigned to the outfield, and only if very good do they get to pitch. As proof, he pointed to 1968 major league pitching rosters which showed only thirteen of 207 pitchers to be black. Such a pattern, extending beyond baseball into other pro sports, suggests a subtle form of discrimination and perpetuates the myth of the strong, but dumb black. As black protests increase, a sense of fear shapes the relations of black and white players. Each side fears the other. Whites sense a black conspiracy and black "tribalism," while blacks charge whites with conspiring to bar them from access to cash and glory.

That blacks have a point is evidenced in the career of Frank Robinson of the Orioles. A triple crown winner in 1966, his dream of earning an extra $30,000 in commercial offers evaporated as he got only a single television appearance and two $500 speaking offers. By contrast, Carl Yastryemski, a white triple crown winner of 1967, rang up an estimated $200,000 extra from such sources. On such evidence rests the black conspiracy theory, and so the conflict between races festers in baseball and in other pro sports.[43]

"It is a sad thing to face," wrote Prentice Gaultt, a black college coach, "but racial prejudice is almost a tradition in sports."[44] But the greatest hurt comes not from prejudice, but rather from the jaded feelings of blacks in sports as they realize that their dream of gaining instant status through sports is a myth. Equally spurious and damaging to all Americans who yearn for a peaceful solution, is the myth that sports can eliminate racism. A cruel sham, this myth seductively promises that if youth play a sport like base-ball they will grow up to practice democracy and equality and to enjoy other blessings of good character. What Americans need to learn is that there are no easy outs from the American dilemma. Only fundamental changes in attitudes can help, and so long as whites are taught to feel superior to blacks, and blacks taught to feel that whites are conspirators, there is little hope for improvement.

A truism for the sports student is that sports only mirror patterns of behavior; they do not shape nor change them. As a social mirror American baseball reflects a nation of factions. True, common values like economic success and love of money and comfort instill cooperation, but even these foster hate and suspicion. In baseball, black and white players continue to belong to competing subcultures which are parts of the larger social structure. Such subcultures are ever-changing, fragmenting, and realigning; thus, the addition of Latin-American players transforms the struggle into a colored versus white, rather than black versus white, confrontation. And complicating the pattern is a black versus Latin-American confrontation.

American baseball reflects this age of racial intransigence. With one group's suspicions feeding another's we encounter a cybernetic loop of suspicion and hatred. And who can say where we are headed? After all, American baseball is a mirror, not a crystal ball. Yet we can learn by peering into the mirror of sports. Above all we see that we are not the fairest of all nations, and we never have been. To realize this is to be liberated at least from the vanity of trying to act like the world's fairest. Perhaps in humility we might deflect our energy and action toward reducing the ugliness that mars the spirit of mankind everywhere.

NOTES

1. Frank Tannenbaum, *Slave and Citizen: The Negro in the Americas* (New York: Vintage Books, 1963), pp. vii–ix, 48–82.

2. Arnold Rose, *The Negro in America* (New York: Harper Torchbooks, 1964), pp. xii–xxxiv, 1–30.

3. C. Vann Woodward, *The Strange Career of Jim Crow* (New York: Oxford Univ. Press, 1957).

4. Alrian Anson, *A Ball Player's Career* (Chicago: Era, 1900), pp. 148–50. *Sol White's Official Baseball Guide, 1907,* pp. 60–128. Also, *Sporting Life,* June 4; July 23, 1884. *New York Clipper,* June 14, 1890.

6. *Sporting Life,* Aug. 9, 1890; *Boston Globe,* April 1, 1897; Ted P. Sullivan, *Humorous Stories of the Ball Field* (Chicago: Donahue Co., 1903), pp. 176–79.

7. Robert W. Peterson, *Only the Ball Was White* (New York: Prentice-Hall, 1970). The book quotes from a 1923 agreement by major league owners to keep blacks out of the major leagues.

8. Reviewing *Sporting News* from 1886 to 1942 shows two references to black baseball. Black children were depicted in the early 1900s under the caption of "coons" watching white teams train in the spring. In 1942 (March 19) Negro fans were pictured again only this time the caption upgraded them to "colored fans."

9. LeRoy (Satchel) Paige and David Lipman, *Maybe I'll Pitch Forever* (New York: Doubleday, 1962), pp. 30–118, 243–45.

10. *New York Times,* June 29, 1973.

11. Murray Chass, "Campanella Recalls Negro League Days," *New York Times,* Aug. 3, 1969.

12. *Baseball Digest,* May 1947, p. 56.

13. *Sporting News,* Nov. 5, 1931.

14. *Nation,* Sept. 17, 1938.

15. Edwin Bancroft Henderson, *The Negro in Sports* (Washington: Associated Publishers, 1949), pp. 179–81.

16. John Brooks, *The Great Leap: The Past Twenty-five Years in America* (New York: Harper Colophon Books, 1968), pp. 285–89.

17. Voigt, *American Baseball* (1970), p. 302.

18. *Sporting News,* March 28, 1946. Henderson, *Negro in Sports,* p. 190.

19. *Sporting News,* April 12, 1945.

20. Quoted in Alfred Andreano, *No Joy in Mudville* (Cambridge, Mass.: Schenkman, 1965), p. 15.

21. *Sporting News,* Oct. 4, 1945.

22. Article by William A. Kunstler, *Life,* July 28, 1969.

23. Veeck and Linn, *Hustler's Handbook,* pp. 211–30.

24. Stanley Woodward, *Sports Page* (New York: Simon and Schuster, 1949), pp. 82–83, 134.

25. A. S. (Doc) Young, "Jackie Opens the Doors—Wide," *Ebony,* Dec. 1968.

26. *Baseball Digest,* July 1957, pp. 60–63.

27. Richard Bardolph, *The Negro Vanguard* (New York: Vintage Books, 1961), p. 453. Young, "Jackie Opens the Doors." Arthur Daley, "The Trail Blazer," *New York Times,* April 9, 1968.

28. Robert Lipsyte, "Politics and Protest," *New York Times,* Feb. 10, 1968; March 10, 1968; Aug. 12, 1968. "Executives—Leading the League," *Time,* July 8, 1968.

29. (New York: Signet Books, 1973), pp. 352–73.

30. Milton Richmond, Syndicated UPI column, April 9, 1968.

31. *Baseball Digest,* July 1957, pp. 60–63.

32. Voigt, *American Baseball* (1970), p. 300, for a summary of Aaron Rosenblatt's study.

33. *New York Times,* June 28, 1973. *Time,* July 9, 1973.

34. *New York Times,* July 23, 1969.

35. Joseph Durso, "Emmett the Great," *New York Times,* Aug. 21, 1966. George Vecsey, "The Man in Blue," *New York Times,* July 5, 1969. *Sporting News,* Dec. 14, 1970.

36. Voigt, "America's First Red Scare."

37. *Sporting News,* Nov. 7, 1970.

38. Voigt, *American Baseball* (1970), p. 305.

39. *Sporting News,* March 6, 1971.

40. Leonard Koppett, "White Sox Franchise in Deep Trouble," *New York Times,* Aug. 30, 1968.

41. Richmond, UPI col., April 9, 1968.

42. Bob Addie, "Hate Hustlers Make 'Hoot' the Way He Is," *Sporting News,* Oct. 26, 1968. Leonard Koppett, "The Unappreciated," *New York Times,* July 30, 1968.

43. Jack Olson, "The Black Athlete," *Sports Illustrated,* Part I, July 1, 1968; Part IV, July 22, 1968.

44. *Ibid.,* Part V. July 29, 1968.

9

American baseball and the union ethic

In the wake of the 1972 baseball players' strike the following comments were gathered:

FANS: The greedy bastards: How could they do it?
                    —Reading, Pa., beer distributor
      The first 400 readers to send in ballots say the strike was not justified.
                                    —*The Sporting News*
                                    April 15, 1972
SPORTSWRITERS: April 1, 1972, will go down as a black date in sports to mark the first general strike.
                                    —Oscar Kahan
                                    asst. Managing Ed.
                                    The Sporting News
      This strike was not for the Hank Aarons . . . or Willie Mayses. It was for the four-year players who pass up college, spend three to five years to make the majors, and have a career ruined by a dead arm or leg.
                                    —Howard Cosell

ACADEMIC OBSERVERS: The strike reveals baseball operations to be a hilariously inefficient cartel.
—Lance Davis and Jim Quirk
Cal. Tech. Economics Dept.

BASEBALL COMMISSIONER: Obviously the losers in the strike action taken are the sports fans of America.
—Bowie Kuhn

OWNERS: Since Mr. Miller has become associated with the players, I've heard nothing but threats. I think the players have been misled by Marvin the Great.
—Charles O. Finley
Oakland Athletics

I don't give a damn if they strike. . . . There can be no compromise from our stand.
—August Busch
St. Louis Cardinals

A GENERAL MANAGER: The players are damn greedy. . . . I'm disgusted with the whole lot of them. This game has been pretty good to them. I think baseball deserves something better.
—Jim Campbell
Detroit Tigers

A PLAYER: Maybe the average fan couldn't sympathize with us. But we thought it was important. The important thing is, we stuck together.
—Frank Robinson
Los Angeles Dodgers

AN OLD TIME PLAYER: I never sent a contract back in my life. The most I ever got was $25,000 . . . they cut me to $21,500 the next year. . . . I think the players are biting the hand that feeds them.
—Enos Slaughter
now Duke Univ. coach

PLAYERS ASSN.: Money is not the issue. The real issue is the owners' attempt to punish the players for having the audacity not to crawl.
—Marvin Miller

PRESIDENT NIXON: [On April 9 he expressed] an interest in a quick settlement.

These rhetorical examples vividly illustrate how baseball's troubles escalated into a strident national issue. On April 1, 1972, major league baseball players embarked on a general strike against the twenty-four club owners over the matter of pension benefits. Before a settlement came thirteen days later, the major league playing schedule was shortened by several games for each team, affecting the outcome of four divisional pennant races, and perhaps of the World Series that year.

While the strike raged, volleys of rhetoric thundered from the positions of both sides. Thin on fact, much of it was confusing, reflecting general bewilderment over each other's motives. Union-busting, power-seeking, salary-gouging, trouble-making, interloping, electioneering (by Nixon)—these expletives described the motivations. Accompanying all this were expressions of horror over the apocalyptic consequences of what was said to be American baseball's first strike. In the player demands some critics saw a reflection of a broadly pervasive dog-in-the-manger attitude that supposedly sapped the moral strength of the nation. Others predicted the death of American baseball, while still others predicted a rebirth. But all such opinions, so leadened with emotion, challenge the student of sports. Although serious students are appalled at the pile of emotion and myth, such materials are useful for understanding both baseball and America.

A bewildering social phenomenon like the 1972 baseball strike affords a dual opportunity for learning about our world. On the one hand it summons one's scholarly imagination to make use of such tools as social history and classic sociology to address an apparently chaotic event and to try to place it in its larger cultural setting. On the other hand, the stridency of the rhetoric mirrors a broad conflict of values and affords a good opportunity to view a social institution in a dynamic setting. The strike shows baseball to be groping for a new equilibrium in this age. In following the two-way path of understanding, the student of sport should gain both insight and skill in his basic task of untangling social issues and sorting values and facts.[1]

PLAYERS VERSUS OWNERS—A CASE HISTORY

That sense of history which the late C. W. Mills judged to be so essential a part of the sociological imagination was in short supply during the 1972 strike. Especially deficient were sportswriters, those ad hoc observers and monitors of the baseball scene, most of whom pronounced the strike to be the first of its kind. From that error, many leaped to a devil theory of its cause, blaming greedy players and their "outsider" leader, Marvin Miller, for igniting the conflict.

But the history of major league baseball shows a repetitive pattern of hostility between players and owners dating back to the establishment of the first major league. Beginning in 1871, the struggle swirled about the issues of pay and power. After 1871 each passing decade saw renewed flareups. As always, the players sought freedom to move where pay was highest, to organize to defend their collective interests and to improve playing conditions. To these classic gripes they have lately added pension rights to their demands. In opposition, owner interests aimed at maintaining their territorial rights and their control over players.

The struggle began with the founding of the first major league, the National Association, in 1871. A player controlled league, its structure allowed players freedom of bargaining, which they employed to good advantage. When the Association folded in 1876, it was an owner's plot that did it in. Charging players with the sins of maldiscipline and profitlessness, the owners set up their own structure, The National League of Professional Base Ball Clubs, and went on to rewrite baseball history by denying all claims of the old Association to pioneer major league status.[3]

But individually and collectively players fought back. In

1882 catcher Charles Bennett challenged the reserve clause in a state court. In winning he scored the first of several such victories on behalf of the players. But always the owners managed to deflect the impact of court decisions and continued to impose the illegal clause. The persistence of this clause, binding a player to a single team, thus became the chief *casus belli* between players and owners.

Collectively players also seized opportunities to regain lost power whenever interloping leagues tried to challenge the monopoly of the National League. In the 1880s two rivals, the American Association and the Union Association, fought for major league status and each began by offering players freedom from the reserve clause. Of course, this was done cynically for the purpose of luring established players, and in the case of the American Association the National League owners promised major league status if the interlopers would sign a National Agreement pledging to keep the clause. Then in 1884 these allies jointly froze out the Union Association in a season long struggle at the gate.

As a class action, the greatest of all baseball strikes was launched by organized players in 1890. Under the leadership of John M. Ward, a handsome, versatile player who in 1890 was at the same time a player-captain, a lawyer, and president of the Brotherhood of Professional Base Ball Players, strike action was taken against the reserve threat and an attempt by owners to hold salaries to a $2,000 maximum. After securing financial backing, the players that year organized and ran their own major league. For a single season the Players National League staged its own race (won by Boston) and outdrew its National League rivals at the gate. But the revolutionary league collapsed when its timid backers withdrew their support in the winter, blaming heavy financial losses.

In crushing the Players' Brotherhood, the victorious National League owners then turned on their American Association allies and ruined that league in an 1891 war of roster raids and price-cutting. Victory gave the Nationals a monopoly which they maintained for a decade and brought the players' cause to its lowest point. Although the hated salary limitation rule was invoked, its impact was blunted as individual owners refused to abide by their own agreement. Many used under the table grants and other dodges to keep star players happy. Yet the overall effect of the national monopoly, in which a single, twelve-club "big league" was set up, was to cow the players until the American League war of 1901–1903 afforded one more opportunity for players to bargain for higher pay and to jump their reservations. An end to opportunity came in 1903 when the embattled leagues framed a new National Agreement which restored the reserve clause in both the major leagues, as the American gained major league status. In 1913 the Federal League incursion mounted another serious challenge to the major league status quo, once again affording opportunity for player independence. But the movement collapsed after the 1914 season, the victim of a closed ranks policy by the established majors.

Although rival major leagues offered the best opportunity for players to regain loss power and to gain salary boosts, such movements were temporary and abortive. Indeed, they were limited to the Mexican League challenge of 1946 and to Rickey's remote threat to launch a Continental League in the early 1960s. More recently, a handful of major leaguers have found playing opportunities in leagues in Japan and Latin America. Altogether these afforded little freedom of movement, and owners moved quickly to fence them off by blacklisting players who turned to them as outlaws. In the case of Danny Gardella, however, who was blacklisted for jumping to the Mexican League, a suit settled out of court to Gardella's advantage exposed the shaky legal ground on which the owners stood.

Yet time would teach the players that the surest road away from serfdom was the union ethic. This meant organizing a union for collective action against owners. The Brotherhood of Professional Base Ball Players was the first such attempt and it collapsed in 1890. Later on in the nineties a player,

N. Fred Pfeffer, tried unsuccessfully to organize the players. And in 1901, the Players Protective Association was formed by ex-players Charles Zimmer and Harry Taylor, the latter a practicing lawyer. Although blessed by American Federation of Labor chieftain, Samuel Gompers, the union floundered and its leaders were discredited by owner propaganda.

Later, in 1912, as the Federal League War broke, major league players organized a third time. Under the leadership of David Fultz, another player-turned-lawyer, the short-lived Baseball Players Fraternity was launched. That year its seventeen demands included the right of players to receive copies of their contracts and the right of castoff players to bargain for re-employment as free agents. These demands and others, including limited severance pay and improved working conditions, were conceded. But the collapse of the Federal League and a rising salary trend during the prosperous 1920s weakened the union. Its quiet demise restored power to the owners, who once again practiced their time-honored divide and conquer tactics, insisting as always on their rights to deal with each player individually. Nevertheless the legacy of the Fraternity included an established precedent for collective bargaining.[6]

As a counterweight to the power of the owners, unionization gained ground after World War II. Early in 1946 the American Baseball Guild was organized under the leadership of Robert Murphy, a lawyer and one time examiner with the National Labor Relations Board. This fourth attempt at unionization of ballplayers drew strength from the Mexican League opportunity for players and the owners' blacklisting response. Striking at the reserve clause and demanding higher pay and better working conditions, Murphy reminded players of their rights to bargain collectively under federal law. The Guild then moved to organize players by teams into chapters, each having an elected spokesman-representative. Many joined, but an abortive test case in Pittsburgh failed to carry off a strike. This crippled the Guild, but owners were fearful, and in the summer of 1946 they met with player representatives and conceded a $5,500 minimum salary, severance pay, expense money, and contract adjustments.

The price for such concessions was the elimination of the Guild as a veto group and the exclusion of Murphy from player councils, In effect, a company union policy was instituted. But the principle of collective bargaining was even more solidly established in baseball. Moreover, the players had scored a portentous victory by winning the first all-out pension plan. An idea first hatched in 1946 by Martin Marion, shortstop of the St. Louis Cardinals, it was widely publicized and eventually supported by four owners, who persuaded the others to agree to the concession. The pension plan went into effect in 1947 and was to be financed by receipts from All-Star games, World Series games, and radio and television income. The pension plan allowed a player with as many as four years' playing time in the majors to draw a pension beginning at age forty-five.[7] A portent of future demands, the pension, with its stress on security, formed the focal point of present-day conflicts between players and owners. And the rising expectations brought on by pension concessions soon prodded players into launching the fifth and present union movement.

Jaded by company unionism, the players formed the Major League Baseball Players Association in the late 1950s. Initially Judge Robert Cannon of Milwaukee served as chief negotiator for the players, but he lacked salary and credibility. His style of "personal diplomacy," with an emphasis on mediation, soon soured the players. Thus, in 1966 the players hired a full time labor representative, naming tough-minded Marvin Miller, a former steel union economist, at a salary of over $50,000 a year.[8]

To the two dozen major league owners the appointment of the flinty Miller was a slap in their faces. Reacting hotly, they forbade the use of pension funds to finance Miller's salary. That stroke forced the Association to charge each player the sum of more than $300 annually in dues. Nor did the owners pass up any chance to bad-mouth Miller, but that

battle-wise veteran remained unruffled and coolly professional. In quick time he forced the owners to recognize his
executive committee of the Association as the players' bargaining agency. Counterattacking, the owners in 1967 named
John J. Gaherin, an executive of the Publishers Association of
New York City, as chief negotiator for their interests. Thus,
each of the embattled groups now owned its own high-priced
negotiator. And challenging the two negotiators was the task
of considering a list of demands drawn up by Miller on behalf
of the players. Heading the list were demands for a sub-
stantial increase in the minimal salary, a challenge to the reserve clause, a proposal for arbitration procedures that would
bypass the Commissioner of Baseball, and a request that
owners consider shortening the annual playing season, which
had expanded to 162 games.[9]

As his clout, Miller had succeeded in uniting the players
behind a 1969 strike threat. When the owners yielded, Miller
scored a victory, winning an increase in minimal salary to
$13,500 and an increase in pension payments.[10] Such suc-
cess opened up another front against the owners as major
league umpires organized and flexed their muscle with a
strike threat.[11] Now thoroughly alarmed, many owners saw
Miller and the Association as the chief threat to baseball's
status quo. Adopting a much tougher stance, the owners stiffened their resolve against further concessions as the 1972
round of negotiations began. Rejecting Miller's argument
that America's inflationary spiral mandated a cost of living
boost in pension payments, the owners refused to allow the Association to use interest money earned by the pension fund
for this purpose. When both sides refused a compromise, the
issue was joined and the 1972 strike followed. The strike
lasted for thirteen days in April and ended with a compromise that allowed $500,000 in earned interest to be added to
pensions. The settlement found both sides claiming victory,
but the shortened season cost owners an estimated $5 million
in lost gate receipts, and the players lost a portion of their
salaries. Moreover, animosities generated by the strike wid-

ened the rift between players and owners, fomenting continuing tensions, and increasing the likelihood of renewed warfare in the near future.[12]

SOME CONSEQUENCES OF THE OWNER-PLAYER STRUGGLE

The sports historian might well choose to stop at this point, but hopefully his sociological imagination will goad him toward further explanations. Certainly, the acceptance of sports studies as a scholarly discipline hinges on the ability of its students to shed light on our understanding of social change, lest such efforts emerge as a merely descriptive form of popular culture.

Viewed sociologically, major league baseball's century long existence shows an institution groping for equilibrium in a changing environmental setting. To know baseball is to understand American social history, especially the history of changing values which prompt structural changes. To attempt explanations will yield impressionistic findings, but the attempt is worth the risk of error.

Above all, the episode of the 1972 strike and its continuing climate of hostility shed light on broader tensions wrought by the acceptance of the union ethic among Americans in all areas of work. When major league baseball began, unionism was in an incipient stage. The union ethic clashed with established notions of economic individualism, and if grudging acceptance was gained in skilled trades, further attempts at unionization were often crushed, creating a strong reaction against the union ethic. Such victories strengthened the beliefs of baseball owners in their rights to control their allotted franchises, to rule players by hiring, firing, trading, and blacklisting, and to enforce norms of behavior by use of salary cuts as sanctions. More often than not, players accepted these, as did other American workers, thus enabling owners to feel that their antiunion philosophy was justified. So long as the mood held, union attempts by ballplayers were abortive. Also, player-unionists dissipated much energy in debating whether to use the Gompers craft union approach or the total union approach of the Knights of Labor, or to take a professional association approach. Similar indecision stymied other workers in American society, notably school teachers. Of course, the professional approach was enticing for its status appeal, but on the other hand, it tended to reject strike action and to encourage players to bargain individually. Thus, on the whole, the professional approach played into the hands of owners who thus continued their divide-and-conquer tactics.[13]

But in time the sobering experience of the Great Depression and the New Deal gave new impetus and respectability to the union ethic. After World War II the militant thrust of unionism cut into many fields of employment, signaling a broad acceptance of unionism in our national life. In time even professional organizations turned to union tactics.[14] That ballplayers, too, would embrace the union ethic was predictable.

In our age a chief goal of the union movement aims at guaranteeing pensions and retirement security. This reflects a major change in American work, testifying to increasing feelings of vulnerability among workers in all jobs and professions. Certainly, baseball players always faced the reality of their sudden and devastating obsolescence. For a long time players accepted being cast off as part of their lot, so that few owners even bothered to inquire about the fate of the men they fired. Today's owners, like other employers, dare not be so calloused, because the problems of unemployment and retirement have become a national concern.[15]

Changing attitudes of ballplayers toward their profession also reflect changing attitudes of Americans toward their work. Like other workers, ballplayers are less bound by feelings of loyalty to an owner or to a club. According to Maurice Stein, this is a natural response to the spread of bureaucracy patterns, a theme popularly treated by Charles Reich in *The Greening of America*, and more precisely by David Riesman's writings. According to Stein, the experiences of 11 million

American soldiers in World War II taught the social lessons of bureaucratic life—of being a number, being thingified, and above all being replaced. For ballplayers the expansion of club staffs made them perceive baseball play as a bureaucratizing experience. It made them see themselves as commodities, capable of being purchased, specialized, managed, motivated, and otherwise thingified. In a word, ballplayers, like many American workers, felt alienated in their work. To counteract such alienation, workers turned to veto groups (usually organized union bureaucracies) for protection. Sociologist Robert S. Lynd caught the meaning of this important trend of our time when he wrote: "We live in an era in which only organization counts—values and causes without organizational backing were never so impotent." More recently David Riesman's notes on the proliferation of veto groups struck the same note.

The quest for bureaucratic efficiency in baseball induced owners and their growing staffs to meet the challenge of changing urban patterns by moving to the newer population centers. Over the past two decades baseball franchises pushed into new urban areas and drastically transformed the structure of the game that had stood stable for half a century. Now there are twenty-four major league franchises instead of the familiar sixteen; and if a location proves unremunerative, a club stands ready to move to a better paying market. With such rapid shifts went new techniques of marketing the game, including transcontinental flights, night games in godsplenty,[16] and television commitments. These and other changes created challenging conditions of adjustment for ballplayers.

Meanwhile the growth of commercialized leisure outlets signaled the spread of a fun ethic in American life. With so many leisure dollars to be harvested, other sports promoters moved in on the old baseball monopoly with their attractive alternatives. Today professional leagues in football, basketball, hockey, soccer, and softball compete with golf, track, and tennis for the spectator's dollars. In each rival spectacle worker-players face problems similar to baseball players. Their answers to these problems have stimulated baseball players to change their attitudes and expectations to match concessions won by other professionals. An expected result has been to raise salaries, thus increasing the tensions between players and owners.

Then too, changing definitions of American individualism affected the lot of American baseball players. Over the past century the American ethic of individualism has proven to be every bit as tough, flexible, durable, and adaptive as the aggregating union ethic. Indeed, individualism grows symbiotically with groupism. For example, black Americans banded together in veto groups to win greater freedom to practice individualism. In baseball this drama and other consequences of continuing individualism are mirrored. Today players demand freedom to be themselves, and in such an atmosphere the reserve clause rankles as an anachronistic symbol of involuntary servitude in America. Along with other workers of today, ballplayers openly challenge the right of owners to dictate behavior patterns, to treat people as property, or to herd them around arbitrarily.

The persistence of the American ethic of individualism is mirrored in the vocal demands of many players that they be allowed to live their own lives, to dress as they wish, to behave as they wish, and to seek comfort if they so desire. The hedonistic thrust of a comfort ethic is another manifestation of individualism, and today's players reflect the trend. Like most Americans players want comfort in marriage and companionate family privatism. This raises a question of familism's impact on player demands and suggests the hypothesis that wives have a lot to do with motivating and supporting the new style of militancy among ballplayers.

That value that encourages Americans to obtain the credentials of formal education, resulting in a mania for college degrees, has affected baseball. As in other areas of work, more formal education leads to higher advancement. Moreover, the better educated worker is more likely to challenge traditional appeals to his loyalty, whether these appeals come from a nation, a school, a firm, or a baseball club. With owners turning to colleges as sources of playing talent, they should prepare to receive more challenges from the ethic of individualism. Thus does the analysis of broad American values promise insights into the changing structure and functioning of a sport like baseball as well as a broader understanding of its total environment.

BASEBALL'S SEARCH FOR A NEW EQUILIBRIUM

Broad cultural changes helped to mold baseball into its present conflicted structure. A full description of baseball's present structure is a project for a meticulous sports sociologist. Here I will only sketch the dimly perceived outlines of a present-day structure of conflict, emphasizing those obvious groups that are involved.

Speaking crudely, baseball's internal system shows the cluster of twenty-four owners with their "hilariously inefficient cartel," embracing twenty-four bureaucratized franchises. Ranged against this group is the players' veto group, the Major League Baseball Players Association with 600 members, headed by Marvin Miller. Tied in with the owners is the office of the Baseball Commissioner, headed by Bowie Kuhn, and regarded by the Players Association as slavishly tied to the owner interests. A third group in the structure of conflict is the organization of baseball umpires with interests similar to the players' but normally regarded by players as antagonists.

The external system includes the amorphous cluster of baseball fans, largely seen as a public, but differentially organized because of special interests and varying enthusiasms. Mediating groups include sportswriters, many, like the *Sporting News* staff, largely committed to owner interests. As professional mythmakers, writers continue to function as interpreters of the game and their stand on matters such as the strikes shapes the opinions of many fans. But writers feel threatened by television interests, whom they regard as rivals in interpreting the game. Because much baseball revenue now comes from television sources, the prospect of losing such revenue in a protracted strike is a major factor in compromise settlements. Unquestionably, the future will see much internal change in baseball coming from television stimuli.

Government bodies, local, state, and federal, exert a major influence because of public investments in stadia and because they administer and judge laws relating to property antitrust laws, civil rights laws, and the like, and because of their necessary sensitivity to public interests. Thus, the problem of creating a favorable public image looms large in the strategies of owners, players, and the Commissioner. Whatever steps are taken by an internal group must account for such environmental concerns. Likewise, gains made by other professional sports affect baseball. The interplay of such influence areas as outlined here should generate many hypotheses for future studies of American baseball.

NOTES

1. C. W. Mills, *The Sociological Imagination* (New York: Oxford, 1959), pp. 77–79.

2. Defined by Mills as "a quality of the mind that will help to use information and to develop reason in order to achieve a lucid summation of what is going on in the world and . . . happening to themselves."

3. Voigt, "Baseball's Lost Centennial."

4. A detailed account of this struggle is in the appendix.

5. Voigt, *American Baseball* (1966), pp. 285, 307.

6. Voigt, *American Baseball* (1970), pp. 67–68.

7. *Sporting News,* April 25, 1946; June 19, 1946; Aug. 7, 1946; May 6, 1972. (Bob Broeg's column). "The Major League Baseball Players' Pension Plan" (Mimeographed paper, Office of Baseball Commissioner, 1967).

8. *New York Times,* June 5, 1966; Aug. 11, 1967.

9. *Ibid.,* Aug. 11, 1967.

10. Robert Smith, "Baseball Needs a New Pitch," *Look,* Feb. 18, 1969; Feb. 15, 1969.

11. *New York Times,* April 21, 1969.

12. *Sporting News,* April 29, 1972; April 9, 1972.

13. Theodore Caplow, *The Sociology of Work* (New York: McGraw-Hill, 1964), pp. 139, 200–204.

14. A. H. Raskin, "Unionism's New Frontier," *New York Times,* May 22, 1972.

15. Leonard Koppett, "Brief Careers of Most Players Called Pivotal Fact in Dispute," *New York Times,* Feb. 19, 1969. See also Lee Allen, *The Hot Stove League* (New York: A. S. Barnes, 1954).

16. Those who study the physical effects of night baseball tell us that daylight play affords a player an average of 1600 units of light to see by, whereas night games reduced these units to 200.

BALL 4

American baseball in a changing society

"Change," Adlai E. Stevenson reflected, "is the master of us all." And today the recognition of this law is the key to survival in American society. For the student of American sports this is much more than a twice-told tale, for the law of change crops up so often as to suggest that the greatest promise to come out of the study of sports is the insights into our changing society. Certainly, many such insights swirl around changes in the American national character.

In this final section a trio of essays probes basic societal changes as reflected in American baseball. The first essay treats changing tastes in American hero worship, revealing a trend away from consensus heroes of legendary proportions to the more realistic, situational heroes of today. That heroes, villains, or fools can be manufactured by image makers to serve the interest of a group is the lesson of the second essay on the umpire as an American villain. And the final essay looks at the important changes in our information media and shows how such changes remold our lives.

10

New heroes for old

In the changing face of American nationalism, popular choices in sports heroes reflect changes in society's values and norms. According to historian Dixon Wecter, as the Civil War fused us into a nation, an accompanying industrial upheaval destroyed the people's sense of community as a fixed place and moved Americans to embrace collective symbols like the Flag, the Constitution, the Declaration of Independence, along with popular heroes to substitute a feeling of national community identity. And under the pressures of industrial growth, popular images of heroes were transformed. Having decisively abandoned royal and aristocratic heroes, Americans took to glorifying the self-made man of the Industrial Revolution. The new pattern deified the myth of the ordinary man rising to the top, an image that reflected a deeply felt hope that the American people really do rule.

This trend toward the democratization of heroes afforded opportunities aplenty for aspiring heroes to emerge out of changes in the social environment. So basic were such changes that most Americans were convinced that they had a share in the hero-making game. However, when a black American like Henry Aaron fails to arouse all-out enthusiasm for his mighty Homeric efforts of today, it suggests that the American social environment is not always ready to accommodate a splendid performer. To make it to the top, the modern hero had to perform the dual trick of adjusting to a changing social environment while conforming to ever-changing values. According to Wecter, this formerly meant being unselfish; having a nickname to lend a common touch; being strong without being the bully; failing now and then so as not to be too successful; and for his ultimate deification, being dead, since living heroes are seldom taken seriously by Americans! In addition, the modern hero had to be human and patriotic—to love his country, to be manly, and to be earthy.[1] Such was the climate of heroes in 1940, and of course, this climate is changing.

Wecter's trail-blazing probe into American hero history has recently been furthered by the work of Daniel Boorstin, whose brilliant analysis sheds light on the state of American heroes of today. Boorstin's book, *The Image*, shows how the communications revolution, by speeding up the production and consumption of news and by making us a nation of television viewers, has given Americans an ad hoc feel for events and personalities. And so we have entered a world of pseudo-events. In a bewildering world of illusion, our increasing consumption of pseudoevents has us devouring news and newsworthy personalities so voraciously that we constantly crave an *ersatz* diet of manufactured news which is planned, planted, and ambiguous. Reflecting a world view of extravagant consumption, it has us thinking that we can partake of everything the world holds and that we can shape our world into whatever forms we wish. Such a view kills our linear sense of history by teaching us to expect a flood of new heroes each new season. So the heroes we now get are manufactured celebrities, here today—gone tomorrow, perhaps well summed up in the TV jingle, "Once around life, once around living."

In the passing of the old style consensus hero, that self-made person who performed in the arenas of politics, business, or the professions, heroes of today come from the world of entertainment, including, of course, the world of big time sports now dominated by the electronic media. This is the world of the pseudoevent, dominated by its illusory images. In this new world, events are *made* as are the celebrities involved in the events. Indeed, God is the ultimate image in our world because He is presumed to be the greatest of all the celebrities! In sports many events are pseudo, although Boorstin thinks that baseball remains linear and factual; but then he wrote before the reorganization of the major leagues into four divisions with the added device of anticlimactic divisional playoffs which so effectively erase the memories of the long regular season campaigns. Nevertheless, Boorstin saw a craving for the old linear sense of history, which is why he thought Americans read the sporting pages more than any other part of a newspaper and why sports fans seem to react so angrily when a sports event smacks of manufactured phoniness.[2]

Complementing the social histories of Wecter and Boorstin is the work of sociologist Orrin Klapp, whose book, *Symbolic Leaders*, attempts to explain the process by which celebrities are made. He likens the process to a tennis match with the would-be celebrity on one end and the consuming public at the other. In serving his image and deeds to the public, the celebrity must become what a fickle public wants him to be. Yet, even when victorious, he wins a momentary victory because he so soon finds himself alone on the sidelines as another celebrity delivers his serves.

In an earlier work, *Heroes, Villains, and Fools*, Klapp shows how a changing American culture admits a confusing variety of norms and lifestyles that make it impossible to get consensus on a hero, villain, or fool. Indeed, Klapp notes fifteen different categories of heroes, villains, and fools, and his study shows how the same person may at the same time be hero, villain, or fool in the eyes of different segments of the public. Moreover, heroes have feet of clay, and villains and fools are likely to be celebrated as heroes. This may make it easier for a modern hero to be himself and to live his own life, but it makes a national consensus on a particular hero impossible to obtain. This ambiguity has led serious writers to ponder the loss of universal standards in our culture.[3]

To the sports historian works such as these suggest fascinating leads. From the beginning major league baseball's history reflects the trend toward the democratization and specialization of heroes. By the decade of the 1880s heroes of all kinds were celebrated in baseball and the siren call of popular worship lured hundreds of young hopefuls to seek to become one of 240 major league players. Those who made the grade were stereotyped by sportswriters and by owners as gullible country boys, endowed with devil-may-care attitudes toward life, inclined to be wastrels, and easily tempted by drink and fleshpots. By 1900 this stereotype was solidly entrenched, enough to dissuade decorum-minded hotel keepers from billeting baseball teams, to convince owners that salaries of ballplayers ought to be minimized, and to persuade moralizers that such men are certainly sinners.

Notwithstanding this negative image, baseball fans saw enough glamor among baseball players to lionize them. After all, ballplayers of the eighties displayed many positive virtues that Americans admired. Spartan heroics was one such virtue and baseball players of that era amply displayed this. An outstanding example was Charles Bennett, a star catcher with Buffalo, Detroit, and Boston, whose stalwart work behind the plate left him with all his fingers deformed. Then, at the peak of his career in 1893, Bennett suffered the loss of a leg in a grisly railroad accident that closed his career in a whirlwind of sympathetic public response.

During this era there were durable heroes whose seemingly timeless performances won for each of them a following of fans. The list included men like Joe Start, whose career began in the 1860s and lasted till 1886. Start was called "Old

Reliable" by affectionate fans. Others like him included "Cap" Anson, a longtime fixture at first base for Chicago, whose dismissal as playing-manager late in the 1890s showered the owners with howls of public protests. Still others included Dan Brouthers, whose career spanned twenty years, and Roger Connor and Jim O'Rourke. So beloved was O'Rourke that Manager McGraw of the Giants brought him back to catch a 1904 game, eleven years after he had retired and when he was in his fifties. That day O'Rourke responded by collecting his last major league hit.

If durable heroes were few, each season produced momentary heroes of remarkable promise. Some, like Charles "Hoss" Radbourne, zoomed to stardom in a single season, as when Radbourne single-handedly pitched Providence to a National League pennant in 1884. And every season saw some youngster, dubbed a "phenom" in baseball jargon, who was eagerly watched until, as usually happened, he burned out like a meteorite.

From the beginning of baseball history fans loved the speedy baserunners whose base stealing exploits made them stars. In the eighties men like Harry Stovey, Billy Sunday, Bill Hamilton, Arlie Latham, and Mike "King" Kelly topped all the others in such skills and were adored by fans. Of these, Billy Sunday, who delivered YMCA sermons on the side, received extra credit for his piety. Indeed, fans admired those players who developed other skills while playing baseball. Harold McClure and Jim O'Rourke earned law degrees during the off season and later entered fulltime practice. So did John Ward, captain of the Giants in the nineties. Ward's versatility led him to direct the Players Rebellion in 1890, and his extracurricular activity also had him wooing and winning a noted Broadway actress, which only added to the mystique of this handsome player.

But the *prima* hero of American baseball's first golden age was Mike "King" Kelly, whose colorful and carefree baseball life made him the darling of fans despite his disdain for sober virtues. Handsome and rakishly mustachioed, Kelly was a feared hitter and all-round player who knew the value of publicity. Once he told a pal that he didn't care what they said about him, so long as it was said. Holding a sports column aloft he remarked, "See what they say about the old man... I am the 'only player.' Why don't some of you dubs break a window and get yourselves talked about?"

As king of players he knew what crowds liked to see, and he gave it to them. As a baserunner he would sometimes feign lameness, then suddenly recover, and steal a base. Often when on base and with the umpire's back turned to him, he would scoot from first to third, cutting across the diamond, precipitating cheers and boos from fans. Playing in the outfield in Boston, he might taunt Irish-American fans in the cheap bleacher seats by pretending to be an Orangeman. And once he amazed a crowd by trudging to his soggy outfield post carrying a heavy board. While his fellow fielders slipped and slogged, Kelly stayed high and dry, laughing at the boos and mudballs thrown at him by fans.

Unfettered by protestant taboos on drink, Kelly never concealed a love for spirits, and his reported sprees only added to his mystique. As baseball's first superstar, Kelly appealed to fans who vicariously identified with his uninhibited lifestyle. In Kelly many found the freedom to strike back against their oppressors, and fans loved reading of the time mentioned earlier when Kelly got the chance to shake hands with President Grover Cleveland and grasped the President's hand so hard as to make him wince.

In 1887 Kelly was raised far above the company of ordinary players when Boston purchased him from Chicago for $10,000. The deal was the baseball story of that century and papers debated it for weeks. So popular did Kelly become that a picture of him sliding into second replaced one of Custer's Last Stand in many Boston saloons. And when the hullaballoo died down, it was clear that baseball fans had chosen their first deity.[4]

Kelly's sudden death in 1894 saddened the baseball world

and left a lonesome gap. Not for more than a decade would another superstar rise to fill the gap. In the meantime baseball underwent a stylistic transformation as scoring strategy shifted to the so-called "scientific game." The new style stressed tight defenses while the offense concentrated on bunting and basestealing to deliver a few runs. Opposing this style was the muscular, "manly slugging game" which produced long ball hitters like Ed Delehanty of the Phillies, but the day of the decisive long-ball hitting game was far off. During the nineties dominant teams like the Baltimore Orioles and Boston "Beaneaters" won pennants by emphasizing the scientific style. The Orioles built a formidable machine, manned by Hugh Jennings, Willie Keeler, John McGraw, and Wilbert Robinson. Using brawling tactics, combined with a mastery of the new style, they unnerved opponents. Their dash and deviltry cast them as heroes in Baltimore and villains elsewhere.

A low profit era, the nineties saw hyphenated Americans, the children of immigrants, rise to stardom to the delight and admiration of their compatriots. As Irish-Americans did in the seventies and eighties, German-Americans in the nineties rose to stardom as their compatriots applauded the deeds of pitchers like Ted Breitenstein and the rising young superstar in the making, Hans Wagner. Henceforth, each decade would see ethnic groups making heroes out of major league players from similar backgrounds. True, ethnic discrimination made the lot of these players difficult, but unlike black Americans, who were barred completely, their path into baseball was open. Perhaps no group suffered taunts so mercilessly as did native American Indians. During one season in the nineties Lou Sockalexis, a Penobscot Indian, rose to brief stardom with the Cleveland team. In a short, but dazzling season in 1897 Sockalexis so delighted Cleveland fans with his hitting that the club was renamed "the Indians." However, response took the form of ear splitting war whoops and stereotyped newspaper gibes such as making the player a relative of Sitting Bull. It was more than Sockalexis could stand. He turned to drink, which only fueled ugly stereotypes of irresponsible red men, and Sockalexis was forced out of the league after a brief season in the spotlight.

Not for generations would ethnic players be freed from the cruelest of gibes about their origins. But over time a necessary tolerance, forced by the power of ethnic veto groups, made highly dangerous such a simple-minded faith in the melting pot myth as this 1908 utterance by baseball writer Tim Murnane: "We got our language from the English and most of our institutions from the Dagos and the Dutch [sic]. But there are two things I teach the boys that are all American. One's the good old flag and one's baseball." [6]

With the restoration of the two major league system in 1903, major league baseball regained a stable, profitable equilibrium. From 1900 to 1920 the scientific style dominated playing strategy and tactics. During this period pitching predominated and such masters as the stylish Christy Mathewson of the Giants, the fast-balling Walter Johnson of the Senators, the spit-balling Ed Walsh of the White Sox, and the ever-victorious Cy Young of Boston reigned as heroes. But the new superstar of the age was an outfielder—Detroit's perennial batting champion, the fiery and determined Tyrus Raymond Cobb.

As a batter Cobb terrorized pitching for twenty-three years and his .367 lifetime batting average rewrote all earlier hitting records. This alone put Cobb at the head of the army of 10,000 major leaguers who performed since 1871, but Cobb's "something extra" included a lifetime total of 892 stolen bases, a triumph of speed and derring-do that made him a most exciting player to watch. Beyond this, Cobb was a driving, combative performer whose very presence stirred fans and players. His zeal for perfection gave him no rest. As the superstar of his age, his daring performance won him alienation and envy. His early years with Detroit were friendless and were marked by bruising fist fights. His closest associates decried his "rotten disposition." Shunned as a rookie, he fought his way into the lineup, disdaining sympathy that might have been his had his detractors known of his hangups, including his deep grief over his father's tragic death and his sensitivity toward his southern origins.

Anti-Cobb sentiment welled up in many ways and made him into a superhero and supervillain—a baseball Jeckyl and Hyde. Taunted by fans and players, he fought back hand-to-hand. Once he rushed into the stands and struck an insulting fan. And his frequent feuds and fist-fights with players incited rumors that he was crazy. And yet he became the idol of a generation of fans, the highest paid player of the age, and the embodiment of those Industrial Age values which applauded the win-or-else spirit. Because he fulfilled these values Cobb towered over the great batters of the day, including the solid, efficient Honus Wagner and the handsome, graceful, flashy Nap Lajoie.

His image projected a mixture of heroics and villainy, a combination that underscores the complexity of American hero worship. For he was the unbeloved hero. No longer, it seemed, could one man embody all of the conflicting values and traits admired by Americans. For now it appeared that only a variety of specialized heroes could cover all of the virtues that Americans admired. And American baseball boasted such variety.

For rural-minded fans there were farm boy types like Wagner, who learned to throw by tossing rocks with unerring accuracy; for romantics, there was the dashing French gallant, Lajoie; for power-lovers, there was the slugging Sam Crawford; for admirers of primitive virtues, there was Indian Jim Thorpe; for southern rednecks, there was the foul-mouthed, illiterate Joe Jackson, once characterized as "Ty Cobb from the neck down." Fans used to love to goad Jackson by asking him to spell simple words, hoping perhaps to elicit his angry reply, "How do *you* spell 'shit.' " Finally, anti-heroes were popular, especially the zany, boozing pitcher, Rube Waddell, or another incredible lusher, "Bugs" Raymond, who could pitch and drink with equal skill.

Had there been no superman like Cobb, the mantle of consensus hero likely would have gone to Walter Johnson, the hard throwing pitcher. A virtuous Kansas farmboy, Johnson went on to win 414 games with the lowly Washington Senators, setting shutout and strikeout marks in twenty years of pitching. Had he pitched for a New York team, the media might have converted him into the hero of the age. As it was, his perennial presence in the nation's capital, where he was the durable star of a lackluster team, enhanced his image as the hero of America's silent majority. Blue-eyed, with blond, curly hair, Johnson endeared himself for his honesty, sportsmanship, and even temper—qualities that many Americans thought to be natural to all.

As a public celebrity Johnson won fame by duplicating George Washington's legendary feat of tossing a silver dollar across the Rappahannock River, a toss of 300 feet. And his happy family life at his Maryland farm, where he spent winters raising Guernsey cattle and Percheron horses, further endeared him. While an active player he met and greeted every President from Theodore Roosevelt to Herbert Hoover, and it was the taciturn Coolidge who summed up Johnson's hold on his admirers when he said, "I am sure that I speak for all when I say that he has been a wholesome influence on clean living and clean sport." [7]

In the wake of major league baseball's "guilty season" which followed the 1919 World Series scandal, baseball owners searched for a popular hero of impeccable virtue to oversee the sport. The man they settled upon quickly became a lofty baseball hero. As baseball's first high commissioner, Judge Kenesaw Mountain Landis embodied the stern, puritan virtues of honesty and retributive justice. As a federal judge, Landis' courtroom showmanship won him a sizeable public following as he struck out naively at the Standard Oil Trust, at pacifists, socialists, and labor leaders, and even at Kaiser Wilhelm II. It mattered little to his adoring following that most of his emotional decisions were overruled, for he had become the stern father figure who could be counted on to raise hell with the people's enemies. As the angry puritan in a baseball Babylon, he became high commissioner at a time when chastened owners wanted desperately to restore public faith in the game. So keeping the game honest became his dedication. As Commissioner, Landis hit at allegedly crooked players, at owners and players who consorted with horse-racing interests or gamblers, and at owners who sought to build huge empires by acquiring minor league baseball teams. Often his decisions were draconian, and not seldom they ignored the civil rights of the defendants. Sometimes they were pure blustering and unenforceable. But the fans loved him and he made good copy for the press.

With the passing of baseball's "guilty season," Landis became a drag upon the owners. But by then he was too popular a figure to jettison. Some bucked him; some called him an "irresponsible despot" and an "expensive ornament." But he continued to be enormously popular with the public, which taught owners the lesson that by empowering a saint, they only succeeded in sullying themselves. In naming Landis' successors, the owners made certain that no commissioner would ever again gain such public popularity. Hence, the Landis legacy was a parade of weak, relatively powerless, and quite colorless commissioners that continues to this day.[8]

But if American baseball's second golden age of 1920–1945 needed a father figure like Landis, it also had room for the greatest of all baseball heroes in George Herman (Babe) Ruth. By middle-class American standards Ruth was the antithesis of Landis. A deprived child, he ran wild in the streets of Baltimore, frequenting saloons and pool halls, cursing, drinking, fighting, and stealing. Judged incorrigible at the age of seven, his parents committed him to a Catholic Industrial Home for boys. There Ruth grew to young manhood, fleshing out to six feet, two inches of muscular brawn, with "a flat nose and little piggy eyes and a big grin" that every ball fan would come to know by sight. As a player, Ruth was a genius. With the briefest of minor league seasoning, he became a star pitcher for the Boston Red Sox. And because he hit hard and long and often, he was converted to outfield play by 1919. Sold to the Yankees in 1920, he proceeded to compile a legendary homerun record as he personally transformed baseball offense from the scientific style into the decisive "big bang" style. Even today, twenty-five years after his death, Ruth's legend weighs heavily on any player who excites comparison. Roger Maris and Henry Aaron would readily agree.

As America's baseball demigod, Ruth's fame was international. By 1930 he was said to be the most photographed of all Americans. A charismatic figure, his dramatic homeruns contributed most to the New York Yankees legend and the New York press never ceased touting his heroics. Nearly everything he did made news, and the press had a hard time whitewashing his off-field antics of boozing, wenching, and pleasure-seeking. His debilitating binges, followed by his promises to reform, constantly redeemed him, as did his kindly gestures on behalf of children. So popular did he become that his 1930 salary climbed to $80,000 a season, much of which he dissipated. In vain did moralizers try to drag him down by questioning the logic which paid a "subnormal giant" more than the President. To such an accusation in 1930, Ruth delighted the nation with his naive reply, saying: "Why not, I had a better year!"

Because he was so unmanageable, Ruth found no secure place in the baseball establishment after his physical powers waned. But his loving public never forgot him. Until his death in 1948 his public appearances drew worshipping crowds. When he died in August, 100,000 fans passed by his bier in the rotunda of the Yankee Stadium, "The House That Ruth Built." [9]

With the passing of Ruth, American baseball never again produced a godlike hero. Indeed, it is debatable if any American institution in recent years has been able to produce a hero of national consensus. Instead, as Klapp has shown, our culture now admits a bewildering variety of heroes, villains, and fools; most of them situational, here today and gone tomorrow. As in other institutions, most baseball celebrities are controversial, heroes to some—something else to others.

To be sure, there have been outstanding, durable performers including players like Lou Gehrig, Joe Di Maggio, Ted Williams, Stan Musial, and Sandy Koufax, whose feats as hitters or pitchers made them superstars. But an age of realistic journalism and merciless publicity has revealed flaws in each case. Williams is a case in point. A vengeful Boston press rode him constantly and sometimes Williams angrily responded by refusing to tip his cap at booing fans or even spitting and thumbing his nose at times. And yet, a decade after his retirement he remains a public hero. As for Di Maggio, twenty years after his active career ended he still earns money by modeling for a New York bank. Yet none of these ever attained the following of a Ruth, and in recent years few players have matched this quintet for sustained public adoration.

Perhaps it is the television effect or the competition from heroes in rival sports and in the entertainment world that has made our age the age of situational heroes. More so, perhaps, it is the modern players themselves who disavow the role of hero, by demanding their rights to live private lives and to be themselves. Whatever the causes, and they need exploring, baseball heroes of national consensus like Kelly, Cobb, and Ruth have been replaced by heroes-of-the-moment like Smokey Burgess, Dale Long, Gene Tenace, Denny McLain, and Wilbur Wood. And the history of the game is loaded with situational fools like Babe Herman, Marv Throneberry, and Joe Pepitone, along with situational and reconsidered villains like the Black Sox, Carl Mays, the damn Yankees of the 1950s, Alex Johnson, and Dick Allen.

From today's vantage point, all the efforts of self-righteous baseball rulers from William Hulbert to Judge Landis to Bowie Kuhn have clearly failed to fit players into a neat mold of decorum. They failed because the institutionalization of individualism, a major theme of our culture today, prompts many players to break out of imposed and puritanical straitjackets. Obvious examples leap to mind. A general one shows up in the acceptance of long-haired players as photos of today resemble those of the 1880s. And free spirited individuals like Jim Brosnan, Joe Pepitone, Dick Allen, and Fritz Peterson abound in baseball today. Their free-wheeling insistence to be themselves has the backing of the rhetoric of the Athletic

Revolution, whose spokesmen now challenge the dogmas of coaches, managers, and owners.

Player protests against arbitrary rules of behavior led directly to the institutionalization of the tough-minded Players Association as a player veto group. And most persuasive is the studied logic of those intellectual players like Jim Bouton and Jim Brosnan who argue that all a player of today wants is to be treated as a human being who happens to have a little extra athletic talent going for him. This is a profound expression of that phenomenon that sociologists call the flight from status. Now widely rooted in American culture, its athletic expression in the writings of Brosnan, Bouton, and Curt Flood tells us much about our changing American character. That baseball players can be helped as individuals by such a demythologizing process is perhaps the most important message in a book like Roger Kahn's *The Boys of Summer*. The book vividly dramatizes the two lives of a ballplayer by contrasting the heights of his first life as a public celebrity with the desolate impact of trying to establish himself in a second life, the life of a player trying to find a new identity after being cast adrift from a career while he is yet young.[10]

NOTES

1. Dixon Wecter, *The Hero in America: A Chronicle of Hero Worship* (Ann Arbor: Univ. of Michigan, 1963), pp. 1–16, 485–87.

2. Daniel J. Boorstin, *The Image: Or What Happened to the American Dream* (New York: Atheneum, 1962), pp. 3–19, 59–61, 183, 254–55.

3. Orrin E. Klapp, *Symbolic Leaders: Public Dramas and Public Men* (Chicago: Aldine, 1964), pp. 7–8, 13–25. Orrin E. Klapp, *Heroes, Villains, and Fools: The Changing American Character* (New York: Spectrum Books, 1962).

4. Voigt, *American Baseball* (1966), pp. 170–79, 274–80, 289–90.

5. *Ibid.*, pp. 266–77.

6. *Colliers*, May 8, 1909.

7. David Q. Voigt, "Walter Perry Johnson." Article in *Dictionary of American Biography*.

8. David Q. Voigt, "Kenesaw Mountain Landis." Article in *Dictionary of American Biography*.

9. David Q. Voigt, "George Herman (Babe) Ruth." Article in *Dictionary of American Biography*.

10. Voigt, *American Baseball* (1970), pp. 284–95. Kahn, *The Boys of Summer*. David Halberstam, "Baseball and the National Mythology," *Harper's*, Sept., 1970. Bil Gilbert, "Gleanings from a Troubled Time," *Sports Illustrated*, Dec. 25, 1972.

11

America's manufactured villain—the baseball umpire[*]

By their heroes you shall know a people. The reverse also seems true. "The villainy you teach me, I will execute and it shall go hard but I will better the instruction," says Shakespeare's *Merchant of Venice*. Thus, it would seem that if certain societal roles and behaviors are popularly despised, to know these would afford a glimpse into our "national character." This deceptively simple proposal promises the rewards of social insights for those willing to become villain-watchers. But, as ever, the complicating factor is trying to explain what one sees.

A case in point is the much vilified American baseball umpire, who in the closing years of the nineteenth century became a target of popular abuse. A strange phenomenon in the annals of villainy, the umpire emerges as a manufactured villain, "a villain by necessity" in Shakespeare's words, thrown to ravenous spectators by shrewd owners who encouraged the fans' ritual abuse as a means of abetting the profits of baseball promotion.

*First published in *Journal of Popular Culture*, Vol. 4, No. 1 (Summer, 1970).

For public consumption at major league parks, the umpire was packaged as a special kind of villain. That villains are different, with certain types serving special purposes, is well established in social theory. In *Heroes, Villains, and Fools,* sociologist Orrin E. Klapp drove home the point that even in nineteenth century America there were varied villains, although not so varied a smorgasbord as we find today. In his lineup, Klapp lists five orders within the animal kingdom of American villains, and the one that best fits the umpire is that of "status abusers and arrogators." Within this order lies a genus which Klapp calls "oppressor types," and under this lies another subdivision called "moral persecutor," so labeled because this type has the habit of abusing power held over subordinates.[1] This model best explains the image of the umpire held by nineteenth century baseball fans. As an oppressor, or moral persecutor, the umpire was seen as a threat to the fortunes of the hometown team or to the splendid performance of a local hero. Since both had off days, disgruntled fans found it salving to blame the umpire. Thus, the umpire became the sacrificial lamb, the villainous blamesake upon whom fans could toss their collective frustrations. As a hate symbol, he still functions as a device for restoring the morale of disgruntled fans.

If Klapp's social-psychological explanation serves to place the umpire in a credible villain mold, it is certain that pioneer organizers of American baseball never intended the functionary to fall to such an estate. From the earliest amateur organizations of the 1840s to the opening of the first major league in 1871, all official rules of baseball aimed at making the umpire the most esteemed member of a baseball club. Indeed, in that early "gentlemen's era" of baseball, most clubs tried to restrict membership to "gentlemen." With such genteel company, it was thought to be an honor to be designated an umpire, since it implied that the honored one knew the rules well enough to make his own interpretations. Naturally, such license also meant that the game lacked a clear codification of rules, so it was not surprising that many protested the fuzziness of these "interpretations." However, in that era of organization umpires had powerful champions, such as the directors of the prestigious Knickerbocker Club of New York, who invoked a set of graduated fines for cursing or otherwise offending umpires.[2]

But the cherished idea of baseball as a rich man's game did not last. By 1870 intense intercity competition spurred commercialism and the winningest clubs used husky proletarians to strengthen their teams. With admissions charged and players paid, the end came to the "gentlemen's era," [3] and with it the umpire's status declined.

For a brief time after the establishment of the National League in 1876 the umpire could still draw upon his former status of gentlemanly expert. Helping to keep the old myth alive was Henry Chadwick, the "father of the game" who used his editorial pen to pontificate on the game's moral mission. Although realist enough to retreat from the lost cause of amateurism, he stoutly opted for retaining the amateur umpire. Arguing that to pay was to demean, he insisted that "no higher compliment can be paid to a member of the fraternity, than to select him to act as umpire in a first class contest, as such choice implies . . . confidence in his knowledge of the rules . . . and in his ability to enforce them resolutely."

Up until 1876, which included the five years of the National Association, Chadwick's views carried weight. During that era, volunteer umpires officiated, guided only by a manual published by Chadwick.[4] While the Association lasted, umpires varied in dress, dedication, and decision-making. To the consternation of fans and players different umpires took different positions, some going behind the batter, some behind the pitcher, while others stood in foul territory facing the batter. Even more confusing was the varied approach to calling balls and strikes, while the difficulty of calling an unseen play led Chadwick to suggest that an umpire ask some "gentleman" in the crowd for his objective opinion! Inconsistency in umpiring was a *leitmotiv* of the Association era, and is illustrated by this matter-of-fact comment about Umpire

Theodore Bromeisler: while "experienced . . . prompt and impartial in his decisions," he called balls and strikes "with unusual strictness." [5]

Even Chadwick admitted that these highly personalized decisions ofter erred, but he blamed players for provoking umpires to err by raucous protesting. A smart captain, advised Chadwick, would quiet his men to insure objectivity. And lest such rational advice fail, Chadwick urged club directors to eject insulting players or spectators.[6]

Not surprisingly, there were times when umpire dignity collapsed in the face of angry assaults. In July 1873, during an Association game in Philadelphia, the umpire "had to be protected from the assaults of the gambling portion of the crowd." Sometimes umpires provoked players as did hot-tempered Bob Ferguson, who accused a lethargic New York Mutual player of being in cahoots with gamblers. Angrily retorting, the player called Ferguson a liar, provoking Ferguson to hit the player with a bat. The incident provoked a mob scene and Ferguson got away with the help of a police escort. But usually players provoked umpires, and during the Association era Chadwick often warned against the "vile habit" of disputing umpires.[7]

With the inauguration of the National League in 1876 umpires faced a new era of adjustment. From the start the new league determined to systematize officiating and began by retaining a professional staff paid at the rate of $5 per game per man. Behind this move lurked the fear that umpires could be bribed: the new league wanted a clean public image to insure its success.

Another step toward professional umpiring came when the League ruled that umpires be chosen from an approved list. A groping move toward uniformity of experience, this led directly to the idea of a salaried staff. First tried in 1882 by the American Association, the plan aimed at silencing arguments over what team might choose the game umpire. Under the new plan, three umpires, each paid $140 a month, were assigned to cover all the seasonal games. And each umpire was ordered to wear a blue cap and coat trimmed with gold cord and buttons. Notwithstanding a later attempt to outfit umpires in white, the early notion of umpires in blue persists in practice and folklore.[8]

The new plan with its good pay lured many applicants. Scanning an early list, a *Chicago Tribune* reporter noticed many "played out ball tossers," and sneered that such men would only hurt the game's image: "the average league umpire is a worthless loafer easily tempted and swayed ... a very unsafe and eminently unworthy person in whose hands to place the arbitration of a game of ball played in the presence of great crowds of ladies and gentlemen."[9]

At least some officials agreed, as evidenced by the bitter arguments over the appointees to the first staff of umpires. Eventually the four $1,000-a-year National League posts went to unknowns. Lacking experience, denied tenure, each soon fell before a harsh League rule calling for the immediate ouster of an umpire at the behest of four clubs. With clubs sniping at the staff only one survived; and the banished A. F. Odlin admitted that the job had lost its glamour:

> I was unaccustomed to appearing before the public, and as soon as the customary and inevitable howls of disapproval arose ... I became more or less nervous and was thus unable to exercise accurate judgment.[10]

Increasing an umpire's frustration were the rapidly changing rules and playing tactics of the 1880s. In that decade hardly a season passed without some change in the balls and strikes pattern. Moreover, pitchers contributed to the bewilderment by introducing baffling curves and trick motions. Since existing rules did not define an illegal pitch, the problem of ruling on the legality of a pitch fell to the umpire. At the same time offensive style changes brought the bunt, the hit-and-run play, and tactics in base-stealing. On the basepaths, daring runners like Mike Kelly of Chicago maddened rival fans by cutting directly from first to third when the umpire's back was turned. In a tough atmosphere for survival, umpires gained little by the preseason seminars arranged by rule-makers who hoped to get uniform interpretations thereby.[11]

By the mid-eighties officials faced a mounting number of trouble cases involving umpires. Obviously the vilification of umpires by players, owners, reporters, and fans was getting out of hand. Underscoring the despised status of umpire were the mob scenes of 1884. After experiencing several, the Baltimore club of the Association installed barbed wire to forestall more. In Philadelphia, League umpire Gunning was mobbed for calling a game because of darkness; while earlier in the same town Billy McLean was mobbed. An ex-boxer, Umpire McLean bore the taunts of loud-mouthed fans until, goaded beyond endurance, he threw a bat which struck a fan. Within minutes McLean was besieged and only the timely arrival of a police escort saved him. The following year McLean faced a repeat of the experience in Cincinnati, with police again arriving in the nick of time.

During the eighties umpires found angry players more menacing, and often umpires were beaten up on the field. In 1884, League umpire John Gaffney suffered a cut eye in a fight with John Ward. The incident prompted officials to impose fines of up to $200 with suspension for similar outrages. But club owners seldom enforced the penalty.[12]

Hopes of improving the image of the besieged profession prompted Umpire Joseph Ellick to write an article analyzing his troubled life. In Ellick's opinion, it was the "kicking player . . . anxious to save face in front of a home crowd," who provoked fans into desiring "to kill you and wish you an unpleasant time in the next world." And events supported the thesis. Certainly players of the eighties were skilled hecklers and were encouraged by owners who often paid their fines. In 1886 Umpire Ben Young wearily testified that Charles Comiskey of the Browns was "a most aggravating player," whose trick of conversing with an aggrieved player within earshot of an umpire took the form of a barrage of "indirect" abuse.[13]

Clearly any workable plan for insuring the dignity of umpires would require the full cooperation of major league officials, owners, and reporters. Yet at no time in the eighties or nineties was this achieved. Indeed owners found umpire-baiting to be quite profitable. Although official League policy aimed at strengthening the post of umpire by increasing pay and granting his right to eject boorish players or fans, enforcement depended on the owners. And in the parks it was evident that owners had a vested interest in acquiescing in the degradation of umpires.

Certainly Chris Von der Ahe, the fat, boisterous "boss president" of the St. Louis Browns, saw no reason to curb umpire-baiters. Rather, he encouraged the practice by paying fines. In this way St. Louis became an umpire's torture chamber while Von der Ahe found that his permissiveness paid off at the turnstile. Nor was his an isolated discovery. In Boston a reporter supported the policy, stating that umpires "are too fully equipped with the foibles of our common flesh to assume the business ... of repressing the hasty passions of others. What's the use of coining a player's unpremeditated damn into dollars and cents when you can do nothing with ... the threats and acts of a mob?" Concluding, he urged umpires to accept abuse as a natural part of the spectacle.[14] Once set, this permissive pattern was hard to change and harder to adjust to. A pragmatic solution of a sort came from President "Nick" Young of the National League, who in 1887 advised umpires to placate local fans by giving "the closest and most doubtful decisions to the home club."

In approving the public right to bait umpires, Albert G. Spalding argued that by harassing umpires fans were exercising their democratic right to oppose tyrants! And in 1897 when umpires protested the ambiguity of the new rules, they were reminded that as employees, they "were not to question their superiors." And in his ghosted memoirs, John J. McGraw claimed that fans of the nineties preferred a rowdy, umpire-baiting style. In agreement was McGraw's Baltimore manager, Ned Hanlon, who advised umpires to accept abuse as part of their role:

> Ball players are not school children, nor are umpires schoolmasters. It is impossible to prevent expressions of impatience or actions indicating dissent with the umpire's decision when a player, in the heat of the game thinks he has been unjustly treated. . . . Patrons like to see a little scrappiness in the game, and would be very dissatisfied, I believe, to see the players slinking away like whipped school-boys to their benches, afraid to turn their heads for fear of a heavy fine from some swelled umpire.[15]

Given a free rein, fans and players made the most of it. During the nineties fights and mobbings mounted and the turnover among umpires soared so high that scarcely a season went by without multiple firings or resignations. By now the practice of "kicking" at umpire decisions was widespread and it contributed mightly to the umpire's vilification. Noting this scene in 1890 a *Brooklyn Eagle* writer sarcastically implied that a good player had to be a good kicker:

> How does the busy base ball player
> Improve each shining minute?
> He plagues the umpires all the day
> Because there's glory in it.[16]

Other writers of the nineties welcomed the umpire-scapegoat as a prop for their stories. Seizing the villain with gusto, they poured forth reams of half-humorous, half-serious abuse. Thus, ace reporters like Tim Murnane of the *Boston Globe* headlined local defeats with phrases like "UMPIRE'S GAME." A *Clipper* writer introduced the umpire as the fan's "mortal enemy," whom "it is the proud privilege of every man seated . . . to hiss at and 'bullyrag' and abuse when he does not especially favor the local club." One who umpires, commented the *Sporting News*, "must have a deformed head." And the sarcastic *Washington Post* writer, Joe Campbell, made a specialty of running lurid headlines such as this:

UMPIRE KELLY FLEES
Women Spectators Smite Him With Their Parasols,
Police Escort Him to the Cars

By such prose as this Campbell probably goaded fans:
"Umpire McFarland, the yellowest piece of bric-a-brac that
ever disgraced Nick Young's staff of indicator handlers, was
responsible for the noisy brawl... after which McFarland,
chattering from fear, fled through the gate behind the back-
stop, and was overtaken by Reilly and McJames, which pair
of Senators bestowed a volley of billingsgate on the head of
the mush-hearted umpire."[17]

In this age other entertainers found salable themes in the
national habit of umpire-baiting. In 1888 it was reported that
John Philip Sousa had scored the orchestral part of a comic
opera with a theme built around the evil designs of a villainous umpire. Written by a Washington newsman, the plot pitted clean-cut Eli Yale, a Giant pitcher, against villainous
Umpire Moberly, who lusted after the heroine Angela, at the
same time scheming to cheat Yale's team out of the pennant.
Embellishing this tired plot were songs with titles like, "He
Stands in the Box With the Ball in His Hands"; "The Umpire and the Dude"; and, "An Umpire I, Who Ne'er Say
Die."

Knocking umpires also inspired poets, few of whom
matched this doggerel effort in the *Washington Critic* of 1886:

> Mother, may I slug the umpire,
> May I slug him right away,
> So he cannot be here, mother,
> When the clubs begin to play?
>
> Let me clasp his throat, dear mother,
> In a dear, delightful grip,
> With one hand, and with the other
> Bat him several in the lip.
>
> Let me climb his frame, dear mother,
> While the happy people shout;
> I'll not kill him, dearest mother,
> I will only knock him out.

> Let me mop the ground up, mother,
> With his person, dearest, do;
> If the ground can stand it, mother,
> I don't see why you can't too.[18]

Umpires generally stood helpless as the everyday prose of writers cemented their image as villainous oppressors. If they fought back, as did Umpire Dunnigan in 1886, assaulting a writer for spelling out his "glaring errors," they lost their jobs. Sometimes they also lost the fight, as in the case of Umpire Jennings, who in 1884 tried to lick a Washington writer for the same reason. Arriving at the plant, Jennings ran afoul of the paper's formidable sports editor, who beat Jennings with a paste pot and threw him out.[19]

Even without pastepots, writers had the upper hand. A headline in the *Louisville Commercial* cried, "Robbed at Mob City—An Umpire's Daylight Crime!" And in 1888, a *Sporting News* writer claimed that Umpire Herman Doscher "has always been a home umpire and every manager ... knows it ... he plays for the crowd, and as a grand stand umpire he is a pronounced success." Indeed, so frequent were such sallies that the official *Reach Guide* in 1890 begged writers to stop baiting umpires; or at least to stop calling umpires robbers![20]

Somehow, someway, enough umpires survived the hostile environment, adapting so as not to go the way of the bison or the passenger pigeon. A handful of adaptive arbiters developed ingenious ways of surviving the troubled habitat. In this era John Gaffney surpassed most in storing up merit and tenure, thereby gaining the uneasy crown of "King of the Umpires." Almost without experience in joining the League in 1884, his reception alerted him to the dangers of the job. Called to work in a crucial game, he nervously suited up in a remote corner of the players' dressing room when an outspoken player blurted: "What do you think Nick Young has gone and done? He's sent down to the rural districts of Worcester County and got a hayseed to come here and umpire. ... He'll be lucky if he gets out with his life."

To defy this grim forecast, Gaffney became a tireless,

imaginative, and efficient worker. Although suspended once for drinking and constantly heckled, he accepted his status as villain, comforting himself with the doubtful assurance that only the riff-raff gave trouble. As an innovator, he raised the status of the profession; even his beating helped by moving officials to enact heavy fines and suspensions for future acts of the kind. Meanwhile his decisions on practical problems of ballgames, such as how to call a ball that goes foul after passing out of the park, became official rulings. In this case, Gaffney's decision was that once out of the park, a batted ball is out of his jurisdiction!

By 1888 sports journals called attention to the Gaffney system of umpiring. They liked his tactic of umping behind the catcher until a runner reached first, after which Gaffney went behind the pitcher for a better view of the action on the bases. For a while others were advised to imitate it, and although finally discarded, it remained a practical solution to the problems of a single umpire.

True, some of his ideas were ludicrous. He once told a writer that the "kicking problem" could be solved by making players pay money to the offended umpire. Gaffney reasoned that no sane player would ever want to enrich an umpire! Perhaps one reason why the suggestion died was that club owners of the nineties habitually reserved money from player fines to finance their annual gargantuan banquet!

Asked for the secret of the success that found him earning $2,500 in 1888, Gaffney explained that he knew the rules, that he followed the ball with "dispatch," that he remained calm among players, and that he studied different styles of base running. He seldom fined and he boasted that in seven years of League work he fined a total of only $300.[21]

As King Gaffney's rival, doughty Bob Ferguson at least held a patent of nobility. Famous as a player and manager, as an umpire he was aloof, stubborn—the archetype of the dictator-umpire. His philosophy was tough minded, nearly the polar opposite of Gaffney's:

Umpiring always came as easy to me as sleeping on a feather bed, and it would come to the rest of 'em if they would stand up and give it out that what they say must go. Never change a decision, never stop to talk to a man. Make 'em play ball and keep their mouths shut, and ... people will be on your side and you'll be called the king of umpires.

Perhaps the Ferguson type deepened the villainous image of umpires; if so, it profited Ferguson, who demanded $1,500 in 1886, which was $500 more than the scale. Asked why, he blustered that he didn't care what others got; he was worth more.[22]

Ranged between the Gaffney-Ferguson extremes were intermediary types like the intellectual Ben Young, whose promising career ended in death in a railroad accident while he was traveling to an assignment. A battler for a respected professional image, Young in 1887 proposed a ten point plan which urged that umpires work in both major leagues, that they each get a year's tenure, that owners be forced to protect them from insults and assaults. For their part, Young pledged that umpires would set high ethical standards, avoiding saloons and the company of players. And such strictures as these dominate the ethical code of umpires of today.[23] Meanwhile in much the same manner Bob Emslie tried to re-educate sportswriters: "If we could only have base ball reporters whose partisanship was mild enough to treat us all alike the game would be greatly benefited in the end." [24]

But in the closing years of the last century all such voices seemed hopelessly utopian. In that era abuses mounted as umpires were cursed, bombarded with beer bottles, and beaten. Perhaps 1897 was the nadir for the profession, since so many that year were harried out. By August, indeed, League president Young was losing sleep over lack of officiating:

I thought I had secured Dan Campbell ... but he begs to be excused from working in the league until the business gets semi-respectable. I would have been in a pretty fix but for the

173

courage of Tom Lynch and Bob Emslie. Lynch is a sick man and he needs . . . rest. . . .

Bob Emslie received a sharp blow over his left lung, and coughed up a large clot of blood. He was advised to rest for a week or two, and was just about to start . . . when Sheridan resigned, Hurst was arrested and Dan Campbell jumped the track. Immediately Lynch and Emslie came to my aid, and I believe I will be able to pull through . . . if Joe Kelly of the Interstate League . . . shows up satisfactorily.[25]

In 1903 came the National Agreement that ended the American League war and established the modern dual major league system. But for umpires there was no immediate peace. In the National League, mob scenes occurred in 1904 as owners and writers continued to use umpires as scapegoats for deflecting the ire of fans. Even in the more enlightened American league, under President Ban Johnson's avowed policy of defending the dignity of umpires, there was a *cause célèbre* in 1901. It came when Manager McGraw of the Baltimore club protested Johnson's suspension of pitcher Joe McGinnity for spitting in an umpire's face. Denouncing Johnson as a "Czar," McGraw triggered a running feud which ended with his defection to the National League.[26]

As before, baseball's early modern era of 1903–1920 had umpires in a state of siege. On one flank fans fired verbal missiles, including curses, boos, and waves of maniacal laughter, coming when umpires were struck by foul tips. By now so familiar was the rite of booing umpires that it found musical expression in a popular song entitled, "Let's Get the Umpire's Goat." [27] And most menacing was the lethal pop bottle; a new artifact, harbinger of America's belching cola age, one launched by a clerk of the St. Louis office of the German consulate in 1907 fractured the skull of Umpire Bill Evans. As the young umpire lay between life and death, President Johnson issued stern orders compelling owners to police their stands or face fines.[28] In retrospect, the Evans beaning was a turning point; henceforth, it was upward for umpires, but only within the villain pantheon! Not for them a heroic status.

Meanwhile on another flank carping newsmen kept up their storied jibes. An extreme example of such flak found a writer using a fan's fatal heart seizure which occurred at a game as inspiration for this headline: "Umpire Klem Kills Innocent Fan." But as usual the center continued to be the worst front, for there umpires faced players. As usual umpires came off second best in the war of swearing, kicking, spitting, and spiking. As a defense, cold comfort came from League advice urging umpires to walk away, and later to file reports— trusting the League to right the wrongs with fines. Gradually the procedure paid off, so that a 1904 study showed that 85 percent of umpire trouble cases involved mere verbal abuse. However, umpires paid a price for their tattle-tale defense, inasmuch as they were being sneered at as "men of the cloth." [29]

Not that an umpire needed to prove his manhood. Stationed behind the plate he daily shared double a catcher's share of bruises and blows, since a catcher spent half of each inning in a shaded dugout while an umpire toiled on without rest. Until 1911 single umpires were assigned each big league game, and because one could not be everywhere, players got away with tricks like doctoring balls, fouling runners, and prancing impudently around bases without touching bags. The impossible work environment ended in 1911 with the reestablishment of the dual umpire system, first tried, then abandoned back in the eighties. [30]

Lacking power and tenure, the working umpire felt his loneliness deepened by the knowledge that at any time the votes of five owners could end his career. Obliged to live lives high above suspicion, most umpires learned to shun the company of owners, players, managers, or fans. A dreary monastic existence this, at least for some it was gentled by marital togetherness. The new king of umpires, Bill Klem, freely acknowledged his debt to his wife, while "Silk" O'Loughlin's last moments on earth testified to the depth of his relationship. Dying of flu during the ravaging 1919 epidemic, O'Loughlin made a last request for another embrace from the wife who lay beside him, stricken with the same disease.[31]

In their harried lives during this early modern era umpires traveled without certain knowledge of their itinerary. Not until the teens did they get travel allowances and always they paid the cost of uniforms and protective equipment. Even today the uniform allowance is inadequate. Yet, the biggest expense was their forfeited dignity. To fans nothing was sacred, certainly not an umpire's name. When an earnest neophyte named Colliflower joined the American League staff, he was cruelly mocked. To stop it, he changed his surname to James—a bad choice, inasmuch as fans took to calling him "Jesse"! Under such conditions survival called for moral athletes, something writer Grantland Rice understood when he urged President Theodore Roosevelt to try umping: "It will curb your rash, head-long stren-u-os-it-ee." [32]

Although Umpire Tim Hurst once rationalized that "you can't beat the hours," the fact was that umpires' pay lagged behind rising player salaries. In 1910 the top umpire salary was $3,000, and that year the National League paid only $25,000 (a sum which included $8,000 in travel allowances) for its total officiating expense. A cheap price, it changed little, so that in 1920 under a dual umpire system, total costs came to only $41,000. Of course, star umpires like Klem picked up extra money for working World Series games, but in 1917 Series assignments still brought in only $650 extra. Emboldened by his fame, Klem in 1918 demanded and got $1,000, but President Johnson stubbornly held the other three at the old $650 rate.[33]

How ironic then that these despised villains should have to carry the integrity of American baseball upon their shoulders! A fact only vaguely appreciated by owners, it took a scandal like the Black Sox affair of 1919–1920 to drive it home. Daily exposed to anger and vilification, it was remarkable that the thin blue line held morally firm. Fascinated by this paradox, writer Hugh Fullerton wondered about the psychological propensity of umpires to err. As Fullerton thought, some gratified their love needs by playing the role of "homers," meaning that they threw close decisions to the home team. Others were "bullheads," powered by self-righteousness into defying crowds. As an example, Fullerton cited Umpire Hank O'Day, who boldly called Fred Merkle out in a riotous 1908 decision that helped Chicago wrest the pennant from McGraw's Giants.

Disliking either stance, Fullerton warned league leaders to mount a close watch since the best umpires had off days in objectivity.[34] But Fullerton was too far ahead of official thinking, and the latter worthies continued to choose models like Bill Klem, who seemed to know the rules. Stubbornly self-assured, ex-bartender Klem awed players with his knowledge and cowed them with fines. As others aped his style, Klem accepted plaudits with pride and arrogance. Not until the twilight of his life did he admit to making mistakes; then he explained that his much quoted "I never called one wrong" really meant, "In my heart I never did." A proud martinet, so self-righteous was he that his claimed purity gave a new twist to the umpire villain image. As a septuagenarian Dean of National League umpires in the 1940s, he wrote a Grundyian code of umping etiquette that included the warning that no umpire should point his *gluteus maximus* at fans when dusting off home plate! [35]

While Klem traversed an Olympic road to official dignity, others took humbler paths to the same goal. For his long service and quiet dignity Bob Emslie in 1919 capped a twenty-five-year career by accepting the first umpire's pension. Meanwhile in the American league, President Johnson's policy of hiring stars like O'Loughlin, Hurst, Evans, Jack Sheridan, and Tom Connolly paid off in respect, making this "big five" famous for leadership and efficient control. Of the quintet only Hurst was fired. Too brusk for such controlled professionalism, Hurst was ousted for spitting in the face of Eddie Collins of the Athletics, and for daring to give as his reason, "I don't like college boys."

Except for Hurst, Johnson's star system worked to elevate the status of umpires. Most outstanding was Connolly, an expert on rules, who retired in the 1940s and won a niche in baseball's Hall of Fame. Also important to the cause was Bill Evans, who retired in the 1920s, leaving a remarkable pamphlet entitled, "The Billy Evans Course on Umpiring." A professional primer for rookie umps, Evans' fifty-one points told how to avoid arguments by practicing diplomacy, by concentrating on the ball, and by avoiding eye contact with players, urging young umpires to take their time before calling a play.[36]

Such advice contributed mightily to the professional approach which in the years since the 1920s saw the establishment of training schools for umpires. Today such schools regularly turn out graduates, men professionalized to the hilt and backed by the combined power of officials and owners, united at last in the common cause of maintaining order in a game now vastly enhanced by the prying eyes of television cameras. Lured by steadily rising salaries, umpires of the present era are comforted by the application of the rule of safety in numbers. Now four men work each major league game, rotating at the various observation points, while six are assigned to cover World Series and All Star games.

True, their rights to organize and to bargain collectively, rights which the spreading "union ethic" brought to players after World War II, are denied to American League umpires. National League umpires have a clearer road, but recently American League president Joe Cronin fired two umpires for their organizing activities. However, court suits and threats of Congressional investigations promise soon to solidify this right.[37]

In an America growing increasingly legalistic, umpires no longer need fear mobbings. If not the laws which protect civil rights and personal liberty, then the spacious, well-policed ballparks have made such scenes as the fan pummeling the late Umpire George Magerkurth in 1940 so rare as to be part of a legendary age. Indeed, so safe is the climate that a woman, Mrs. Bernice Gara, in a *cause célèbre* for women's equality, fought and won a right to essay a professional umping career. Having won a *cum laude* degree from an umpiring school and overcoming a problem of securing a proper chest protector, she battled in the courts to win her right to officiate. However, following a single outing in a minor league, she resigned, protesting bitterly the hostility of fans and her fellow umpires. And if in the aftermath most of the umpires opined that umping is no career for a woman, this male judgment is by no means certified as gospel.[38]

Today's baseball scene makes it appear that fans are finding it difficult to play the century-old game of umpire-baiting. But lest it be supposed that the umpire has escaped his villainous status, abuse continues. It takes the form of ritualized booing every time a team of umpires is announced, and mocking jeers still debate close decisions, while cheers ring out when one is struck by a foul tip or otherwise discomfited. Such rites are painful enough, but when national celebrities support the ritual, it hurts more. Thus, when General Douglas MacArthur remarked that Americans must ever defend freedoms, like their right to boo umpires, Umpire Larry Goetz laid aside the late general and searched for a new hero.[39]

NOTES

1. Orrin E. Klapp, *Heroes, Villains, and Fools: The Changing American Character* (New York: Spectrum Books, 1962), pp. 50–67.

2. Dr. Daniel Adams recalled his days as Knickerbocker president in *Sporting News*, Feb. 29, 1896.

3. Voigt, *American Baseball* (1966), pp. 14–22.

4. Chadwick's *Baseball Manual, 1870–1871*, pp. 56–63; 37, 65–66.

5. *New York Clipper*, April 15, 1871.

6. Chadwick's *Baseball Manual, 1870–1871*.

7. *De Witt's Baseball Guide, 1871*, pp. 18–37.

8. *Constitution and Playing Rules of the National League ... Official, 1876*. (Philadelphia; Reach and Johnston, 1876), pp. 5–44. *Spalding Guide, 1878*, pp. 1–23; *1879*, pp. 92–96.

9. *Chicago Tribune*, July 30, 1882; Oct. 8, 1882.

10. *New York Clipper*, March 10, 1883; June 8, 1883.

11. *Sporting Life*, April 22, 1883. Two decades of rules changes and tactical changes are reviewed in *Spalding Guide, 1896*, pp. 160–62.

12. *Sporting Life*, Oct. 8, 1884; March 18, 1885.

13. *Sporting News,* Nov. 6, 1886. For Young's complaint, see *St. Louis Globe-Democrat,* April 27, 1886.

14. *Sporting Life,* Oct. 29, 1884.

15. Hanlon's comment is in the *New York Clipper,* May 25, 1895.

16. *Brooklyn Eagle,* July 26, 1890.

17. *Washington Post,* July 26, 1897; Sept. 13, 1897. *Boston Daily Globe,* July 8, 1892; July 11, 1892; Aug. 9, 1897. *New York Clipper,* Nov. 27, 1884. *Sporting News,* July 23, 1889.

18. *Chicago Tribune,* Aug. 15, 1886.

19. Chadwick, Scrapbooks, II, 69.

20. *New York Clipper,* Aug. 16, 1884. *Sporting News,* July 21, 1888. *Reach's Official Baseball Guide, 1890,* pp. 38–40.

21. Voigt, *American Baseball* (1966), pp. 189–91.

22. *Detroit Free Press,* June 5, 1887. *New York Clipper,* Jan. 2, 1886.

23. *Sporting Life,* Nov. 30, 1887; Sept. 6, 1890.

24. *Ibid.,* Oct. 24, 1896.

25. *Boston Daily Globe,* Aug. 9, 1897.

26. *Reach Guide,* 1902, pp. 36–37. *Sporting News,* Aug. 3, 1901; Aug. 31, 1901.

27. *Spalding Guide,* 1909. William Burnett, *The Roar of the Crowd* (New York: Potter, 1964), p. 38.

28. *Sporting News,* Sept. 19, 1907.

29. *Ibid.,* June 29, 1911. James M. Kahn, *The Umpire Story* (New York: Putnam's, 1953), pp. 107–17.

30. Kahn, *The Umpire Story,* p. 75. Ty Cobb, *Busting 'Em* (New York: E. J. Clode, 1914), pp. 70–91.

31. Kahn, *The Umpire Story,* pp. 216–23. *Sporting News,* Oct. 16, 1919; Feb. 8, 1923.

32. *Baseball Magazine,* June, 1948, p. 36.

33. Kahn, *The Umpire Story,* pp. 120–21, 219–20. U.S. House of Representatives, *Organized Baseball.* Report No. 2002, 82nd Congress, 2 sess., 1952, pp. 1321–25.

34. John J. Evers and Hugh S. Fullerton, *Touching Second: The Science of Baseball* (Chicago: Reilly and Britton, 1910), pp. 181–95. *Sporting News,* Aug. 21, 1924.

35. Kahn, *The Umpire Story,* pp. 77–89.

36. "The Billy Evans Course on Umpiring" (Privately published in 1926. Copy in the Spalding Collection, New York Public Library). *Sporting News,* Dec. 21, 1910.

37. *New York Times,* Sept. 18, 1968; Sept. 20, 1968; Jan. 8, 1969.

38. *Sporting News,* July 15, 1972. NBC, "Today Show," June 30, 1973.

39. *Sporting News,* April 5, 1969.

12

The changing dimensions of American baseball

Unlike biblical days when the coming of spring was viewed as "the time when kings go forth to war," many Americans have found in major league baseball a moral equivalent and peaceful substitute to martial behavior. As a drama of victory and defeat, major league baseball is geared for displacing aggressive urges. As a team sport it glorifies individual acts of heroism, reflecting our mania for individual success. Beyond these psychological props, the long baseball schedule cools the losers by promising an endless string of tomorrows. And if the game piously stresses fair play, sportsmanship, and abiding by rules, it also tolerates cleverness, trickery, and deceit so long as these artful dodges only bend the rules. Thus, the psychological massage of American baseball has taught people to displace aggression by providing a catharsis for hostilities, and a talisman for coping with some of the bewildering changes of the electronics age.

Among the buffeting changes of today none is so portentous or so little understood as that which has transformed our ways of getting and processing information. A wrenching change, this so-called "communications revolution" affects all industrial societies and passes them from a mechanical culture to an electronic culture. The result is a cataclysmic impact on the way we view the world. As Marshall McLuhan explains, the old era of mechanical culture lasted roughly from 1500 to 1900 A.D. and saw printing dominating our information flow. In this era individualized consumption of books and newspapers provided information. By speeding the flow of printed information, the mechanical culture allowed the spread of industrial urbanism and the growth of nation-state societies. In its effects on individuals, the print medium created fragmented personalities; in great variety to be sure, which seemingly promised greater individual freedom. On the other hand, print also allowed a state to control the behavior of individuals. Hence, by chaining personalities to national values and norms, the age of print was reasonably safe from anarchy.

Then came the new electronics revolution to change the mechanical cult of the printed word. By introducing devices like the telegraph, telephone, radio, and television a new social order appeared in the making, one that seemed to be "retribalizing" mankind into a single world "family." Television accomplished this by "immersing us in a whirlpool of information," by presenting events in a manner that encouraged far more active and extensive participation of individuals than the mechanical revolution's medium of print ever did. Indeed, to use the electronic media is to experience feelings that go far beyond the simple sight involvement of print. As McLuhan explains, the medium is the massage, and electronics media touch all of our senses.

The total sensory involvement made possible by the electronics revolution prompted McLuhan to pronounce this new phase as one of the most sweeping revolutions in human history. It will, said he, do no less than create a new mankind; something not overly alarming since mankind has already experienced several such revolutions in his three million or more years of existence. But whenever such a transformation occurred, it was hell on those caught in the middle. To be trapped in between communications revolutions, such as the transition from a linear, print-oriented world of communication to the new electronic world of communication, can have a staggering psychological impact. It is frightening to be told that our linear world of familiar beginnings-middles-and-endings is passing, for it relegates traditional views of history, progress, and reality to the scrap heap. If McLuhan is right, the new electronic era already challenges us by offering a world of "happenings." The passing of the old linear world threatens to end the comfortable equilibrium of unity and continuity that comes to us through such familiar social forms as the nation, state, locality, and neighborhood. Instead of viewing our existence as a function of the interplay of such familiar forms, we will submerge our personalities in a common regard for "the human race." This is a revolution in community. Traditional boundaries, traditional diplomacies, traditional communities, traditional personal histories all will disappear—to be replaced by temporary social alignments of people with momentarily similar interests, whose clashes with rival alignments will lead either to better accommodations or to extinction.[1]

Despite his millennialist imagery, McLuhan's vision turns attention to an area of human behavior too long ignored, namely man's information needs and the means and processes whereby he meets those needs. By stressing the stimulating impact of communications media on our behavior, McLuhan draws attention to a side of human behavior largely ignored by scholars. Whether or not scholars will agree with McLuhan, they must take seriously his attempted interpretation.

Students of sports can find good leads in McLuhan's writings. The potential significance of his theories can be demonstrated by working some of his ideas through baseball history in order to see how the flow of baseball information shifted with the changes in the media. Indeed, baseball never has been a static spectacle. Over the past century the major league game was constantly molded and reshaped to meet changing tastes of fans and changing opportunities for promoting and profiting from the transmission of baseball information. Thus, to review the dynamics of baseball information transmission is to glimpse something of the total impact of America's communications revolution.

An important accompaniment of that revolution has been the multiplication of outlets for transmitting and receiving information. In American baseball the proliferation of information outlets is reflected in the four dimensions of baseball. All are interrelated and each feeds back on the others; yet each in its own right is a baseball environment. First, there is the game as played at the major league parks; second, the game as displayed in newspapers and sports journals; third, the game as presented by radio; and, fourth, the game as presented by television. Each dimension offers a different version of the game, but each version has its own claim to reality. Thus, to know what major league baseball means to a fan, one must first know how he gets his baseball information. A deceptively simple prospect, it is complicated by the fact that a fan passes through more than one dimension. Hence, one must be prepared for confused reactions resulting from a mixing and blending of the four dimensions in the minds of fans. To grasp this point is to begin to understand why so many fans at a ballpark insist on listening to the same game on a transistor radio or why some fans find televised games hopelessly dull, yet consume newspaper accounts of games with insatiable appetites. Baseball is not a simple, closed, boundaried spectacle, but rather a complex, open one. In the light of such a realization any questions about baseball's supposed decline in popularity must be answered by a probe into the four dimensions of the game. Are all declining at once? At any point in baseball history it is possible to show one dimension in decline and another on the rise. And so the history of American baseball reflects the great revolution in communications that over the past century transformed

America into a national community, and, if McLuhan is right, is now working to mold the world into a global community.

Like the young American nation that gave it nurture, major league baseball first flourished in a two dimensional communications world. In 1871, the year the first major league opened play, baseball information could be gotten at the ballparks or in the newspaper columns. This typified McLuhan's mechanical stage of communications evolution. It was a newspaper-dominated world of printed words, and it fostered a symbiotic relationship between major league baseball and the press.

Not surprisingly the earliest baseball centers appeared in cities where newspaper coverage was available. With the coming of the first professional league in 1871, the most profitable and stable franchises were located in Boston, Philadelphia, New York, Washington, and Chicago, where press coverage was plentiful. These centers also boasted the largest ballparks, some capable of housing throngs of 10,000 or more. Usually the early parks were wood structures surrounded by wooden fences. Inside the enclosed area a prominent pavilion shaded the expensive seats while most of the others were in an open grandstand area. In the 1880s double-decked stands replaced the single-storied pavilions, but a park's seating capacity seldom exceeded 15,000. A famous exception was the Philadelphia Phillies' ballyard. Built in 1887 with seats for 20,000, this "palace park of America" boasted double-decked galleries and the most comfortable facilities for players and fans anywhere.

What made all such parks obsolete was the construction in the years 1909–1915 of concrete and steel structures such as Forbes Field in Pittsburgh, Comiskey Park in Chicago, Brush Stadium (later the Polo Grounds) in New York, and Shibe Park in Philadelphia—each capable of seating more than 30,000 spectators. Spurring the building boom was a surge of public enthusiasm for big league baseball, a wave of interest that convinced owners that 3 million fans a year was the expected norm for paid attendance in each major league. Soon afterwards, American League attendance topped the 5 million mark, but by the early 1920s the boom crested. It culminated with the opening of Yankee Stadium in 1923, a structure capable of seating 73,000. Today still another building boom is under way, stimulated by attendance prospects of better than 10 million fans a year. And the suburban location of the new parks testifies to the regrouping of America's populace and the suburban growing edge of our population boom.[2]

The continuing strong current of popular support for American baseball testifies to the attraction of the sport, and bears out McLuhan's point that the media technology creates its own world of demand. In attracting fans over the past century most successful baseball promoters deliberately or accidentally applied this principle. During the game's golden age of the 1880s promoters catered to the horse and carriage set, and during the bicycle boom of that era, bikes were accommodated. The great ballpark building boom of the early part of this century was planned with trolley and subway access in mind. And if the parks built during that period lasted long, few owners envisioned the not-too-distant day when auto traffic would render them obsolete. Thus, by 1923 every major league park was hurting for auto parking space. Yet, today, if McLuhan is right, the auto too is becoming *passé*. Thus, by failing to take account of the principle that technology creates its own world of demand, today's owners may be condemning today's plush parks to quick obsolescence.

Viewing the inside of a park where the game is played offers further evidence of technology creating its own world of demand. The familiar seats with backrests were installed in response to popular demand for comfort, and the widening of the seats after World War II came in response to the increasing physical growth of Americans. Meanwhile our increasing use of food as oral gratification found every park patrolled by a small army of concessionaires, hawking a bewildering variety of goodies during the course of the game. For whatever its symbolic meaning, it is worth noting that these purveyors, like the contingents of park police and ushers, far outnumber the players, and sometimes even outnumber the fans.

Well under way by the 1880s, this trend was stimulated at some parks by the sale of liquor and by the popularity of hotdogs and bottled soda pop everywhere. Meanwhile fans took to sideshows such as music, games, giveaways, fireworks, and the ever available gambling opportunities.[3] Such familar extras as these were developed in the 1880s by promoters like Chris von der Ahe of the St. Louis Browns, who raced horses, dogs, and bikes and who also encouraged brawling on the field by his players because it stimulated spectator interest. Even earlier, Harry Wright had understood the importance of byplay when he introduced the familiar pregame batting and fielding practices so familiar to fans ever since. With men like Wright and von der Ahe showing the way, baseball's first dimension grew lustily. Today owners are ever alert to the need for byplay, and modern hustlers like Bill Veeck developed many such incentives. Today's enticements include food, music, varied programs, and electronic scoreboard gimmicks aimed at families and fans of all ages. Far from trivial, these are considered essential to profitable promotion.[4]

Matching the dynamic growth of baseball's first dimension was the second dimension—the game as played in the daily newspaper. Indeed, it is unlikely that the first could have grown so rapidly without the support of the newspaper dimension. From the time the first major league game was played in 1871 to the 1930s every major league attendance breakthrough was stimulated or accompanied by increased newspaper coverage of games. Coincident with baseball's golden age of the 1880s was a newspaper trend of using specialized sports departments. And the new star in this print galaxy was the scribe who covered games, printed box scores, kept records on teams and players, and ran columns of "inside dope" on the daily movements of teams and players.

Because the major league game was promoted as a "linear

187

sport," with a daily schedule of games extending over eight months of the year, the news media blended nicely with baseball's established pattern. According to McLuhan, the print medium typified the mechanical culture of the "Gutenberg galaxy" of information transmission. As a "hot" medium, the information passed by newspapers appealed primarily to the eye. By limiting its appeal to a single sensory organ this medium tended to fragment the interests of its readers and to herd them into diverse interest groups whose horizons were limited by the printed material that caught their eyes, alerted their interests, and forged their opinions. Despite its obvious limitations, the newspaper dimension is still a potent influence in our lives. With its linear emphasis on beginnings and endings the printed word still shapes our perceptions, as evidenced by our continuing dependence on books and journals.[5]

Baseball's long marriage to newspapers affords interesting insights into the meaning and portents of this phase of the communications revolution. Most significant perhaps is the way news coverage shaped the sense of history for baseball fans. Given the linear style of communicating, the newspaper medium became the "massage" for millions. It taught baseball fans to view a season's campaign in linear logic. There was a spring buildup and training phase; followed by the breakaway phase as teams jockeyed for early advantage; then a midway phase, usually coming in July when front runners were conceded the ultimate victory; and climaxed by the stretch drive phase in September when contenders fought desperately to scale the heights. After this came the World Series phase which proclaimed the year's champion, followed by the hot-stove-league phase when readers were able to review the history of the completed campaign and to find grist for gossiping about players, trades, and speculations about the next year's campaign. To read such fare year after year gave a reader a linear "feel" of history. It was a logic system that allowed a reader to compare any season's play with any other, or any team with another, or any dynasty with earlier dynasties. To be nurtured on this kind of information diet was to have one's perception of baseball shaped by the very medium that transmitted the information. Thus, for generations of fans the sports page was both message and massage.

Given wide support, the newspaper dimension of baseball also created its own technology. Thus, by the 1880s national sporting journals like the *Sporting News, Sporting Life,* and to a lesser extent the *New York Clipper* devoted most of their pages to baseball coverage. Such journals fed dedicated fans plenty of "dope," as inside accounts of players, their records, and their recorded behavior came to be called. Baseball's second dimension also spawned numbers of "guidebooks," such as the *Spalding Guide,* official organ of the National League, and the *Reach Guide,* its American League counterpart. By the twentieth century a dozen such guides had appeared, accompanied by directories, official league publications, and a spate of books—biographical, autobiographical, narrative, and fictional—all on baseball, its teams, and its heroes.

Being a medium of high personalization, the sports pages not suprisingly fostered baseball's "star" system. The newspapers of Chicago and Boston played up the colorful Mike Kelly, the swashbuckling outfielder-catcher, and turned him into baseball's first superstar. Likewise, newspapers of Buffalo and Detroit immortalized a quartet of stars, Dan Brouthers, Dave Rowe, Jim White, and Hardie Richardson, as the "Big Four" of the 1880s. Later the press churned out the living legends of the "old Orioles" of the 1890s by playing up the deeds of John McGraw, Willie Keeler, and Wilbert Robinson. But the powerful New York press soon outshone all others in the business of star-making. Beginning in the late 1880s with Giant stars like John Ward and Buck Ewing, Gotham writers made superstars of McGraw, Ty Cobb, and Christy Mathewson early in this century. Later the same god factory made a demigod out of Babe Ruth and high order angels out of lesser Yankees and Giants and Dodgers.

A century of this kind of ink-stained enterprise produced a parade of manufactured heroes, villains, and fools. It was sportswriters who made folk villains out of umpires, out of the "Louisville Crooks" of the 1870s, and out of the Black Sox of 1919. Among the many players turned into public fools by enterprising writers were pitchers Rube Waddell of the Athletics and the heavy-drinking "Bugs" Raymond of the Giants. Others included the unlucky "Bonehead" Fred Merkle of the Giants, and such ludicrous fielders as Babe Herman of the Dodgers, Zeke Bonura of the Senators, "Marvelous Marv" Throneberry of the Mets, and Dick "Dr. Strangeglove" Stuart of the Phillies. So long as newsmen served up baseball information, such typings were woven into the linear tapestry of baseball information where they fired the fans' imaginations.

Not surprisingly the second dimension also made stars of sportswriters. With bylines and columns going to outstanding writers, fans followed these heroes, eagerly awaiting their words. In the early years of baseball, Henry Chadwick, prolific baseball writer for leading dailies and journals, and editor of the leading guides, became the first writer-celebrity. While Chadwick's active career spanned half a century, he was rivaled by men like O. P. Caylor of the *New York Herald*, Will Rankin of the *Clipper*, Francis Richter of *Sporting Life*, and Tim Murnane of the *Boston Globe*. When these titans departed early in this century, their ranks were filled by new writer-celebrities like the poetic and romantic Grantland Rice, who sang of sports like a Southern Pindar; or Ring Lardner, a pioneer in realistic sportswriting, and Hugh Fullerton, whose forte was inside exposés. This trio appealed to a wide public, but those fans who craved figures and statistics were always fed—first by Chadwick and Jacob Morse, and later by Ernie Lanigan, "the figure filbert." [6]

Knowing the value of free publicity, baseball owners accommodated writers at their parks, perhaps not always elegantly because writers constantly complained about bad press facilities and invasions of their places by friends of the owners. To get even, writers blasted owners in print. In time even friendly owners felt the critical stabs of reporters whose endless searchings for "inside dope" prompted inquiries into tabooed areas like the business and politics of major league baseball, or the psychology of player morale. Stung by critical barbs, a few owners questioned baseball's marriage to the press. A hot debate swirled around the question of whether or not press coverage of baseball games hurt the gate receipts. Certainly the presence of newspaper telegraphers incited such fear, and a few Luddite owners banned the telegraph from their parks when they noticed the large crowds which swarmed around the windows of urban telegraph centers awaiting postings of late scores. Almost no owner sensed that telegraphy was a harbinger of a major communications revolution. In speeding the flow of news, the telegraph fed instantaneous reports to the public. Its effect on newspaper reportage was to push newspaper makeup into a "mosaic-like" mold (the phrase is McLuhan's). Thus, newspaper telegraphy gave a hint of the coming breakup of the familiar linear mold.[7]

At times the opposition of owners to free press coverage was shared by working newsmen who resented the free coverage papers gave baseball. Over the last century writers and publishers have engaged in long hours of debate with clubowners over who was exploiting whom. In retrospect a lot of heat has been wasted on a false issue, since each faction needed and used the other. In a perceptive book on the history of sportswriting, the late Stanley Woodward sampled opinions from a number of circulation managers and found nearly unanimous agreement that sports coverage, especially baseball coverage, sold newspapers. Their overall estimate was that a quarter of all big city dailies were bought by sports fans who savored feature stories dealing with events and heroes as much as they did news coverage of the games. Not surprisingly, the circulation managers told Woodward that they would gladly devote more columns to sports coverage.[8]

Had McLuhan been on hand at the beginning of the debate

between owners and sportswriters, he might have warned that the real threat to the equilibrium of each side lay in the modest, incipient development of electronics media. Had he done so half a century ago, he would have been called a nut. And yet, the new revolution that soon pushed major league baseball into a third, and then a fourth dimension, had begun even before the birthdate of the first major league. The harbinger of the new era of information was the telegraph. Since 1848 the device was revolutionizing news processing by forcing faster and more frequent press runs and speeding the flow of information until news regularly raced ahead of editorial judgment.

From its beginning major league baseball's marriage with newspapers was affected by the rising new medium of telegraphy. But if clubowners never understood its psychological significance or glimpsed its ability to create human interest by instantly involving fans in the drama of a game, it was because owners saw the medium only in terms of its possible threat to gate receipts. His vision clouded by dollar signs, no owner could see in the clipped, terse prose of telegraphic accounts of baseball contests a sign of a coming predominance of the "Marconi Constellation," so soon to eclipse the "Gutenberg Galaxy." This cosmic rhetoric of McLuhan's implies that Americans were abandoning traditional dependence on mechanically produced print media like books and newspapers, in favor of the electronically produced information that radio and television soon would provide.[9]

Radio's evolutionary link with telegraphy was evident by its early name—wireless telegraphy. Following early experiments by Marconi at the turn of this century, the new medium proved itself as an information medium in the areas of shipping and military communication. After the first World War radio's potential as an entertainment medium was exploited so swiftly that American consumers, dazzled by the prospect of hours of free entertainment, lined up to buy receivers. By 1929 most American homes had radios and their ready willingness to buy the products hawked by radio advertisers proved the profit potential in the medium. Thus, radio grew fat on advertising so that by 1929 it had become a billion dollar industry. As rival networks battled one another for the fattest advertising contracts, baseball owners found themselves wooed by network representatives. What the networks wanted and would pay for were rights to broadcast baseball games. Although some owners were fearful, for the usual reasons, early experience showed that far from hurting baseball's basic dimension, the new radio dimension strengthened and popularized both the first and second dimensions.

Of course its social effects were far more profound. McLuhan's principle of a medium functioning as a massage found the new radio medium serving baseball fans an image of the game that was psychologically different from that of the ballpark or the sports page. For many, listening to a broadcast of a ballgame was an intense emotional experience. Many listening fans were stirred by the dramatic voices of announcers who took them into storied worlds where players performed heroically and accomplished deeds far beyond anything a fan might witness at a park. To sustain this psychological drama was the task of a new expert, the "sportscaster." Among the first of the tribe was Graham McNamee, who won fame as a World Series broadcaster in the 1920s. With his rich voice and vivid imagination McNamee shaped the image of baseball's diamond drama for millions. Nor did it matter that he personally knew so little of the game, or that a realistic newsman like Ring Lardner disgustedly mocked his versions. Men like McNamee outdistanced their critics and were joined by later heroes like By Saam, Mel Allen, Harry Heilman, Red Barber, Dizzy Dean, to name only a few. Broadcaster heroes all, they became gurus to vast audiences who often viewed them as having magical powers over the outcome of the game they were broadcasting at the time.

To compare them with witch doctors is a debatable analogy. In McLuhan's scheme, the psychological relationship between broadcaster and listener allows the former to become a manipulator of the latter's emotions. By extending the sense of hearing, radio listening functions as a high-intensity communicative experience, forcing the listener to use his imagination to fill in the verbal scene outlined by the broadcaster. Quite obviously, the more verbally beguiling a broadcaster's account, the more stimulation is giver to a listener's imagination. In the language of magic, the best broadcaster was a superb *shaman*, a magical leader who evoked the most vivid baseball trances for eager listeners.

In a creative essay entitled "Confessions of a Retarded Tiger," writer Bil Gilbert described his personal psychological reaction to large doses of radio baseball. As a youth Gilbert was hooked by an announcer who regularly took him off on trips to a mental wonderworld of heroic baseball. According to Gilbert, radio baseball in the 1930s produced many such fans, listeners whose baseball information came mainly from radio. "Radio—mysterious, disembodied, vivid as a dream—screamed for a fantasy response." Leading Gilbert on his illusory trip was the rich baritone voice of sportscaster Harry Heilmann. In Gilbert's fantasy, Heilmann was in full charge of the scene; thus, at times young Gilbert found himself praying to Heilmann for a Detroit Tiger victory and for a splendid performance by his favorite Tiger hero.

In his solitary listening, Gilbert fashioned a fantasy image of the Tigers at play, deifying pitcher Tommy Bridges and second baseman Charley Gehringer. Even when not listening to a broadcast, Gilbert easily invoked Heilmann's presence in his solitary play, thus summoning up the entire familiar, mystic scene. At such times Gilbert would imitate Heilmann's voice while playing a major league game of his own, tossing a ball on a roof or throwing stones at targets. In such private games, as he allowed his beloved Tigers to crush rivals, Gilbert escaped from many harsh realities into the wonderworld of play. Nor was Gilbert's play a unique invention, as many others of his generation did the same. Indeed, as a boy I often imitated the voice of By Saam, the syrup-tongued broadcaster who did his phoney best to glamorize the forlorn

Athletics and Phillies of the 1940s, in my private major league games played by batting stones at trolley stops in Hershey, Pennsylvania.

Personal experiences aside, radio was an important tribalizing experience for American fans. After all, there were many listeners to Heilmann and Saam. Yet radio domination was a short-lived phase of an ongoing communications revolution. After World War II, television came in with a rush, offering a fourth dimension of baseball information. For many fans, television's realism destroyed the fantasy world of radio. To Gilbert, baseball as played on television, like the game played at a park, never matched the fantasy world of radio. He thus became a "baseball retard," who henceforth carried his mental impression of baseball forever frozen in the radio imagery of the 1930s. As Gilbert put it: "Thereafter baseball was never again serious. . . . The trouble is that it is very hard to have bigger-than-life imaginary playmates when smaller-than-life, but photographically accurate models of the real thing are living-room intimates." [10]

As television destroyed Gilbert's image of baseball, so it affected other fans of the 1930s and 1940s. In retrospect, radio had functioned to destroy the linear sense of history for many as it created the impression that baseball really began with the radio age. In this way, older baseball dynasties, like the pre-1920 Pirates, Athletics, and Red Sox, were forgotten, as radio spotlighted the deeds of the Yankees, Cardinals and Dodgers, new dynasties of the radio age.

For baseball owners the radio medium offered new problems and opportunities. By 1933 owners were involved in contract negotiations with radio networks over the exclusive rights to broadcast World Series games. Three years later the Gillette Safety Razor Company paid more than $100,000 a year to sponsor the games, and individual clubs also dickered for broadcast rights to their regular season home games. By 1939 the smallest sum any major league club received for its home game broadcasting rights was $33,000, while the Giants collected $110,000 a year for its rights.

If such income was a windfall to depression-starved owners, some found it bewildering to have their club linked with the sales of gasoline, cigarettes, beer, drugs, or breakfast foods.[11] More distressing was the impact of such broadcasts on the minor leagues. By the end of World War II major league owners faced an alarming decline in minor league attendance that was linked with the broadcasting of major league games. In this way radio contributed to the shrinking of the minor league network, a network built up over the years at considerable expense to major league owners, who were using the minors as farms for growing future players. Obviously the radio profit windfall was both blessing and curse, although it is unlikely that any boycott of radio broadcasts of big league games could have saved the minors. After all, major league baseball was not powerful enough to stem the tribalizing impact of radio. Also, the thrust of this tribal trend was national, not local. That fans now preferred the major league scene over the small town minor league scene merely reflected radio's capacity to bind the nation into a single tribe.

Today radio is overshadowed by the fourth dimension of television. Nevertheless, like the game played at the parks or in the sports pages of newspapers, radio remains a viable medium for imparting baseball information. The popularity of the highly personal transistor radios and auto radios has fixed the medium's place in a cybernetic loop in which baseball information flows four ways.[12] Today it is the television arc of the loop that offers owners their greatest challenge and most hopeful opportunity for future growth.

Major league owners entered the fourth dimension in 1946, the very first year of the postwar television boom. At first fans flocked to taverns and bars to watch telecasted games, but family sets proliferated so rapidly that by 1951 an estimated 3 million family set owners watched the dramatic playoff between the Dodgers and Giants, while an equal number viewed the contest in barrooms. One can only speculate how a confirmed drunk, like old-time Giant pitcher Phil Douglas, would have reacted to being told that television could have placed him in a million bars at the same time! Be that as it may, from the start owners were intoxicated over the profit potential in television.

Certainly televised sports programming was a deep running vein of gold. Once exploited, the vein proved endless. In 1967 sports television accounted for 796 hours of major network time.[13] And because summertime was a slack time in television programming, baseball's position as one of the few "live shows" of the summer proved strategic. Recognizing that baseball was the "only game in town" in summertime, television networks conceded ever more lucrative contracts, until by 1966 baseball's television income amounted to 27.5 million dollars a year.[14]

But there was still the piper to pay, or if you prefer, the Catch-22 in baseball's affair with TV. For one thing, it quickly became evident that televised baseball was a different game. Soon evidence was added showing how quickly the medium had become the massage!

In McLuhan's scheme, television is the brightest star in the "Marconi Constellation." Today it is the most potent medium in the ongoing communications revolution. Unlike radio or the newspapers, television is a "cool" medium which makes the viewer use all of his senses while actually becoming a participant in the event being viewed. More than any communications medium so far, TV broke the linear sense of history so important to the making of American baseball into a sports spectacular. Before TV, major league baseball was presented as a straight line history, with beginnings and endings, causes and effects, all arranged in a familiar linear pattern. For a century of baseball history the season's progress seemingly flowed that way and reporters by necessity told it like that. In McLuhan's words: "The characteristic mode of the baseball game is that it features one thing-at-a-time." During any game, "timing and waiting are of the essence," and older fans learned to store statistical information of past performances of players to verify the outcome of the waiting game.

By drawing on such mental stockpiles, old-time fans could predict what might happen in present situations, given the same set of data. A familiar habit of thought and action, this style was not limited to baseball; for long years it was the approved world view of the Gutenberg Galaxy. But now television threatens to overshadow this world view, and with it old ways of experiencing baseball.

Television's threat to baseball's traditional image stems from the ability of the medium to involve viewers in deep, extensive participatory experiences. By finding one's self placed in the very center of the game, a viewer fancies himself a participant. Seductively teasing all of the viewer's senses, television makes a viewer fill out the image "by a convulsive sensuous participation that is profoundly kinetic and tactile." [15] Given television's primacy among information media today and its continuing deployment for in-depth monitoring of all kinds of social events, McLuhan predicts the passing of the linear world view of perceiving reality. Of course, McLuhan's critics say he goes too far, saying, after all television does not stand alone, but is in a symbiotic relationship with other media.

Nevertheless there are indications that TV is destroying the linear sense of history for baseball fans. In 1969 the *Sporting News* polled readers, asking them to name candidates for memberships on all-time, All-Star teams. Interestingly, fans responded by naming mostly present-day players, ignoring those of the pre–radio or TV eras. For example, Philadelphia fans named mostly players who were active since 1950 to the all-time Phillies all-stars. Ignored were great Phillies of the past whose records far outshone the moderns.[16]

Other examples bear witness to the upsetting process whereby TV destroys the old linear view. One need only recall the shocked feelings registered by fans when owners relocated major league franchises after 1952, or the horrified gasps accompanying the recent decision to expand the major leagues to include four divisions of six teams each. Such actions by baseball officials shattered a familiar image of a stable major league structure hallowed by half a century of tradition. For many fans, the franchise shifts and expansion programs were a cruel reminder of the transitoriness of everything. But the promise of lucrative television contracts for relocating in new urban centers like Atlanta, Oakland, and Kansas City persuaded owners to buck tradition and to ride out protests from old-time fans.

In subtly reshaping the structure of major league baseball, TV interests also came to control the scheduling of games and the conduct of play. Today TV has much to say about league schedules. By imposing network programming demands, TV made for an increase in night games. Special demands now include the televising of Saturday afternoon and Monday night games on nationwide television. But the most dramatic example of television's power over baseball came in the mid-1960s when the Columbia Broadcasting System purchased the New York Yankees. The controversial purchase raised alarms and alerted Congressmen interested in antitrust violations. But recently CBS disposed of the Yankees to a more orthodox group of owners so that the specter of outright control of ballclubs by television networks was shoved into the background for the time being at least.[17]

Half devil and half angel, television also struck fear into the peripheral peoples of baseball. Dispossessed sportswriters, whose status seemed lowered as that of telecasters rose, attacked the medium for damaging the game. Angrily, writers chided TV sportscasters for their lack of baseball knowledge. In rebuttal, TV men charged writers with jealousy born of frustrations over their coming obsolescence. But this was mere byplay; nothing could halt television from spreading major league telecasts into every region of the land. Like the older radio invasion, the popularity of the new medium gave the minor leagues another body blow, this time so felling that outright subsidies from major league owners were needed just to keep some minors running. As a result a recruiting of talent revolution is afoot which has major leagues looking to college baseball teams for new talent, or like the Kansas City Royals running creative talent seeking and training programs. So if television killed the minors, did it not partly redeem itself by providing in itself a superb device for training young players? Certainly TV facilitates the teaching of baseball techniques in depth and in great clarity, something that all the old books, guides, and instructional devices could not do.[18]

Nevertheless, tremulous owners wondered if the same TV blow that crippled the minors might strike the majors. As an "open medium," TV is fickle and opportunistic. It focuses on many events and has been known to abandon them once the drama has been milked out of them. As long as any drama, baseball included, proves attractive, the big eye of TV is interested. Should it flag or fail to pay; should it prove dull[19] compared with a spectacle like soccer, TV like a virago might go elsewhere. Since other sports attract viewers, some in greater numbers than the baseball following, that dubious old myth of baseball's being the national game has become a cruel joke. Yet baseball owners may at least take comfort in knowing that the cool TV medium treats all sports with the same mercenary spirit. From this owners are learning the lesson of the TV age—that is, that no drama or sport "has it made." Like other dramas, baseball must work at sustaining public interest, not only for the big eye of TV, but in all of its dimensions.

Perhaps players caught this lesson before owners did, since players quickly came to understand how ruthlessly TV could raise a man to celebrity status and then drop him. In an age of TV, heros, villains, and fools as social types come and go. Thus, the medium plays havoc with the great man theory of history by substituting a passing parade of momentary, transitory types. Under the eye of TV it is unlikely that a Kelly, a Cobb, or a Ruth could rise to stardom and stay there for a decade or more as chief idol. What makes this dream so far-gone now is that TV is eternally seeking after fresh events and new heroes. And yet the medium has enabled more players to bask momentarily as situational heroes. Moreover, the medium has enabled all players to be better paid for their services. But the psychological lesson that players seem to have grasped is to prepare one's self for a fast letdown and quick oblivion.

Because they better understand the fickleness of TV fame, modern players seem better adjusted to the medium's caprices than those linear-minded fans who bemoan the passing of old-fashioned baseball heroes. More than ever before today's player is likely to ask, "What's in it for me?" As one of them put it: "Ballplayers resent being scapegoats, symbols, and story material rather than normal men with a little extra athletic talent." [20]

To label today's players nonheroes only echoes the same charges being leveled in other areas affected by the electronic revolution. This would include literature, the movies, the magazines, the military, where nonheroes abound. In sum, the electronics age is not the time for classical heroes in baseball or elsewhere. Had the Reverend Billy Graham understood this, he might not have chided President Nixon for overlooking the Resurrection when Nixon complimented the Apollo 11 crew for "accomplishing the greatest feat since the creation." Indeed, Graham might have understood why a Catholic college voted John and Bobby Kennedy ahead of Jesus in their list of heroes.[21] Who knows, Graham might not have cozied up to Nixon in the first place had he known of the coming of Watergate.

Whether the communications revolution bodes well or woe depends on the faith of the reader. Man makes his own myths and must live with them. And man's media have always helped to shape the world of myth. To change the media is to change man's world view, and when this happens, we may expect a change in the very nature of man. We have seen that

American baseball's passage into the electronic era has unleashed vast changes. And if baseball can be upset and challenged by such changes, perhaps it is time to seek to know by what other means, and in what other institutions, the communications revolution has been reshaping our humanity.[22]

NOTES

1. Eric Norlen interview with Marshall McLuhan, *Playboy,* March 1969.

2. Voigt, *American Baseball* (1966), pp. 90–96, 288; (1970), pp. 43, 94–101.

3. William B. Furlong, "Out in the Bleachers Where the Action Is," *Harper's,* July 1966, pp. 49–53.

4. Voigt, *American Baseball* (1966), pp. 138–39, 208–9. Veeck and Linn, *The Hustler's Handbook.*

5. Marshall McLuhan, *Understanding Media: The Extensions of Man* (New York: McGraw-Hill, 1966), pp. 203–14.

6. Voigt, *American Baseball* (1966), pp. 192–203.

7. *Ibid.,* pp. 99–105, 197, 205, 210.

8. Stanley Woodward, *Sports Page* (New York: Simon and Schuster, 1949), pp. 35–45.

9. McLuhan, *Understanding Media,* pp. 206, 249, 252–57.

10. Bil Gilbert, "Confessions of a Retarded Tiger," *Sports Illustrated,* July 28, 1969.

11. *Sporting News,* May 27, 1943.

12. "The Distant Message of the Transistor," *Time,* Nov. 24, 1967. "The Radio in the Auto," *Literary Digest,* July 9, 1932.

13. Voigt, *American Baseball* (1970), p. 304.

14. "A Locker in the Living Room," *Time,* Oct. 20, 1967.

15. McLuhan, *Understanding Media,* p. 314.

16. *Sporting News,* July 5, 1969.

17. Stanley Frank, "Corrupts! Debases! Exploits!" *TV Guide,* Feb. 4, 1967, pp. 6–11. *New York Times,* Jan 4, 1973.

18. Woodward, *Sports Page,* pp. 207–10. "The Golden Age of Sport," *Time,* June 2, 1967.

19. Jack Craig, "Baseball A Dull Show on TV," *Sporting News,* April 3, 1971.

20. Voigt, *American Baseball* (1970), p. 294. Robert Lipsyte, "Something Less Than Gods," *New York Times,* Aug. 17, 1968.

21. Tom Wicker, "In the Nation," *New York Times,* July 31, 1969.

22. McLuhn, *Understanding Media,* p. 245.

22. McLuhan, *Understanding Media,* p. 245.

Strike 1

When hard pressed, today's major league baseball players have demonstrated a readiness to strike against clubowners. To some baseball observers with limited historical perspectives, such behavior is seen as a radical break with baseball tradition. To set the record straight, this final essay surveys the granddaddy of all baseball strikes that took place way back in 1890.

The revolt of the
baseball players

After crushing baseball's first major league in 1876, the leaders of the National League struggled to discipline players by blacklisting and expelling alleged troublemakers. Under President Hulbert's tough regime, drinkers and gamblers were targets of a cleanup campaign aimed at persuading fans that the National League was determined to maintain a high moral tone in baseball, even at the cost of profits. At first players submitted, but when owners invoked a reserve clause to restrict their mobility, players reacted hotly. To many players the reserve clause, by binding a player to a single club indefinitely, was a thinly disguised plot to lower salaries.

Proof of the suspicion loomed large in 1885 when the owners announced their intent to limit player salaries to a $2,000 ceiling. In defense, the owners cited a threat to baseball profiteering in high salaries, some as much as $5,000 a season, paid to stars.

At first player retaliation took the form of individual protests. In 1882 the brilliant catcher, Charles Bennett, filed suit against an attempt by the owners of the Pittsburgh Alleghenies to reserve him. When the club filed suit against him for breach of contract, Bennett fought back in the courts and won. The decision, the first of several against the reserve clause, branded the clause as lacking in equity.[1]

In 1884 another star player, John Montgomery Ward, in a thoughtful letter to the *New York Clipper*, attacked the legality of the entire owner position. Ward noted that certain players had been expelled for jumping to the Union Association, an abortive major league, that tried vainly to establish itself in 1884. When that luckless circuit failed, many players suffered at the hands of vengeful National League and American Association owners. Charged with contract jumping and reserve clause violations, some were barred for life. In defending these accused, Ward argued that he was only urging player rights to legitimate contracts. In conclusion he counseled players to disavow the highhanded reserve clause.[2]

To the *Clipper* reader accustomed to frothier baseball prose, Ward's letter was unusual, but then Ward was no usual player. Born in Bellefonte, Pennsylvania, in 1860, he attended Pennsylvania State College, where he starred in baseball. After brief seasoning in a semipro league, he joined Providence in the National League in 1877. Two years later, in an age of one man pitching staffs, he literally pitched Providence to the league pennant. But the effort strained his arm and threatened an end to his pitching. Ward, however, resolutely trained himself to play the infield and switched to shortstop. The change increased his tactical knowledge of the game, prompting the new owners of the New York Giant franchise to name him their captain in 1883. As a strategist and advocate of the "scientific game," Ward practiced and taught switch-hitting along with the fine points of baserunning and place-hitting. By 1888 his reputation grew, buoyed by his book, *Base Ball: How to Become a Player*, which an editor called "the best and most exhaustive treatise that has yet appeared on the subject of our national game." [3]

Beyond this Ward was a natural leader. Although unbeloved, he was admired and respected by his men. Most were awed by his boundless energy that prompted him to attend Columbia University law school during winters and to graduate with honors in 1885.

Equally admirable was the handsome Ward's lifestyle. In 1887 he astounded the theatrical world by wooing and winning the hand of one of the most noted actresses of the day, the beautiful Helen Dauvray, after a secret courtship that titillated Victorian hearts. Unhappily, the marriage became one of Ward's failures. Its dissolution in 1890 had an impact on the Players League strike because in an unusual coincidence Ward's sister-in-law had married Tim Keefe, a Giant pitcher and Ward's chief lieutenant in his unionist activity. With Ward's divorce suit pending, resultant tensions between the brothers-in-law undermined their mutual trust.[4]

That such a man as Ward should have shouldered the task of protecting his fellow players was an act of altruism unusual in the dog-eat-dog world of baseball. One searches in vain for some ulterior motive. True, the highly paid Ward stood to lose heavily if the owners succeeded in limiting salaries. But his obvious baseball genius, his celebrity status, his career as a lawyer, surely gave promise of a future fortune to be made. Be that as it may, Ward chose to shoulder the thankless and profitless task of organizing and masterminding a player rebellion. Perhaps he thought himself to be the only player capable of carrying it off. At any rate, under his guidance the Brotherhood of Professional Base Ball Players was organized on October 22, 1885. The meeting produced a statement of principles and a clarion call for action:

> We, the undersigned, professional base ball players, recognizing the importance of united effort and impressed with its necessity in our behalf, do form ourselves this day into an organization to be known as the "Brotherhood of Professional Base Ball Players." The objects we seek to accomplish are:
>
> To protect and benefit ourselves collectively and individually.
>
> To promote a high standard of professional conduct.
>
> To foster and encourage the interests of . . . Base Ball.[5]

Once established the Brotherhood grew rapidly. Its astute sponsors wisely recruited players before confronting the owners. Over the next eighteen months Ward and Keefe visited each team, listening to arguments against joining the Brotherhood and doggedly dispelling them. From such visits came the idea of forming a Brotherhood chapter at each local team, with local leaders reporting to the Brotherhood's central committee. Thus, in May 1886, Detroit joined, adding an eleven man chapter, followed quickly by chapters from Chicago, Kansas City, and St. Louis. Before the year was out Boston, Philadelphia and Washington had thrown in, so that by early 1887 the Brotherhood claimed 107 members. Not until 1890, the year of the strike, were Association players recruited, and in that year thirty joined.[6]

The success of the Brotherhood movement owed much to a cadre of respected and clever players. In 1889 Ward and Keefe were joined by Dan Brouthers at the executive level. In several cases, moreover, star players headed local Brotherhood chapters. Such men were magnets in attracting rank and file players. Moreover, fans were impressed by the Brotherhood's organization. With Ward handling publicity, the movement curried public approval. And solid support came from the editors of *Sporting Life* and the *Sporting News*, the latter's editor praising the "live organization" for its noble aims and noting that: "Only the most intelligent and best-behaved members of the profession are eligible for membership, and, there is no room in the ranks for chronic disturbers or lushers." [7]

For the most part sporting press opinion favored the Brothers. Thanks to Ward's selling job, only four well known sportswriters opposed the movement and three of these were on the League's payroll. On the other hand, respected writers like Frank Richter of *Sporting Life* and Tim Murnane of the *Boston Globe* acted as Ward's advisers. Given open channels by sympathetic sports editors, Ward used them tellingly; in letters and articles he struck blow after blow at owner policies. While much of the material was propaganda, some of the articles raised important points about the lack of equity in American baseball. And a few of these were so portentous that half a century later a Congressional committee studying antitrust violations in baseball used them for guidance.[8]

Ward's chief targets included the reserve rule, the blacklists and unequal contracts. When the famous $10,000 Kelly sale of 1887 dramatized the new practice of selling players, Ward attacked the sale in an essay entitled, "Is the Base Ball Player a Chattel?" By impressive logic Ward argued that such was the case, noting that the sale was made without Kelly's approval and without Kelly's getting a portion of the selling price. To humanize such transactions Ward argued that owners be obliged to consult with players before reserving, selling or disciplining them. A simple plea for equity, but it was wholly unacceptable to owners.[9]

Fighting back, the owners tried to divide players among themselves and to separate the players from their public support. Sometimes they used trickery effectively. At the annual meeting in 1887 when the players sought to get owners to recognize the Brotherhood, the players expected a turndown. To their surprise the owners greeted the petitioners and listened to proposals for a new contract, and "then consented to modify the old contracts." Indeed, the owners promised to liberalize policies on suspensions, expulsions and blacklistings, and to eliminate the half dollar assessment for players' road expenses. In return owners asked the Brothers to back owners in curbing drinking, gambling, and dishonesty among players. Yet, in the all important matter of the salary limit plan owners refused to reject it in writing. When Ward persisted in his demand that this be done, owners directed their arbitration committee to do so, but that body met a few weeks later and failed to do so.[10]

However, that bit of chicanery failed to dampen a mood of friendly trust between owners and players that ran through 1888. Although Cassandras on both sides warned of sabotage, such voices were drowned in a sea of cheers for Spalding's upcoming world baseball tour. Already America's leading sporting goods tycoon, Spalding was the leader in owner councils. When his entourage embarked in October 1888 with Ward in tow, baseball's labor front seemed secure. But Spalding was a master at turning giddy minds to foreign triumphs. With Ward out of the way, the League officials announced that the salary limit bill would go into effect in 1889 with no player getting more than $2,500, and only a score of men getting as much.

The announcement shocked the leaderless Brothers. Ward was abroad, under personal contract to Spalding, and could not return until March 1889. Forced to wait for his return and to bite the bullet, the Brothers took courage in Keefe's grim remark: "Won't Ward and the others be mad?" [11]

But Ward met the challenge coolly. When the ship docked, he quit the tour and launched a retaliatory campaign. Rejecting a strike for 1889, he used a dual strategy. On the one hand he organized a grievance committee to treat with the owners; on the other he directed each chapter to seek financial backing for an 1890 players major league. Any question as to Ward's personal preference became academic when the owners flatly refused to treat with the Brothers. That ended all hope of compromise. Hardened by Spalding's duplicity, Ward issued an ultimatum: not only must the owners end the salary limit scheme, but they must also halt all sales of players. Failure to do so would lead to an all out strike. When the owners failed to reply, the season of 1889 moved to an end with two armed camps openly planning each other's destruction in the season to come. Astonishingly, the 1889 season still produced a lively National League race with Ward captaining the Giants to a second straight pennant victory.[12]

But the end of 1889 saw the front of battle lower. As owners prepared for their annual meeting, the Brothers met and heard Ward's keynote address laying the blame for the coming conflict squarely on owners whose "dollars and cents" mentality perverted the game into an "instrument for wrong." In later sessions the players organized a Players National League and drew up an eight point plan assigning each player to a team, pledging each team to finance a $25,000 operational fund for the league. Each player was assured a salary equal to his 1889 figure and a share of all team profits above $10,000. If any team made more than $20,000 everything over that amount was to go to less fortunate clubs or else be equally divided among all players. Thus, Ward made it clear that the new league was to be truly a Players League, as players were given key posts on the board of directors, and the majority of stock shares were also to be held by players.[13]

With financiers, officials, managers, players, and even white clad umpires in fold, Ward seemingly left nothing to chance. Except for extending the pitching distance to fifty-one feet, the playing rules were the same as the National's. Understandably, Spalding's firm was cut out of equipment sales as the new league adopted the "Tim" Keefe ball, a product of Keefe and Becannon's sporting goods firm. All things considered, the Players League was shipshape enough to confront the National owners with the most serious threat in their history.[14]

To meet the threat the National owners massed their power. As alarms sounded, the owners replaced their bumbling, ornamental president, Nick Young, with a war committee headed by Spalding, John Day, and John Rogers. It was a trio of business-minded realists, with Spalding the chief genius. His personal motto, "Everything is possible to him who dares," typified Spalding's ruthless spirit. And Spalding thrived on dares. As a pitcher, he had promoted the first overseas baseball tour. Two years later, in 1876, he pulled off the coup that brought on the National League and ended player control of American baseball. At the peak of his playing career in 1876, he ended his career to plunge into sports equipment manufacturing. With his brother's help and an $800 stake, he opened a Chicago plant. Fourteen years later he was a millionaire and by 1890 he was busily organizing a sporting goods trust. In time that venture would require all his effort, so that he would quit National League councils, but in 1890 he was the owners' chief and he was fiercely anxious to preserve what he had wrought.

In marshaling his defensive forces, Spalding struck in many directions. To counteract wholesale player defections, he ruthlessly raided American Association rosters, defying the National Agreement that protected against such incursions. Indeed, moving further he lured two strong Association clubs, Cincinnati and Brooklyn, into the National League. That his latest coup reduced the Association to a minor league hulk bothered him not at all. And his similar raids on lower minor leagues afforded opportunities for young, hungry players to make the majors. For many of those men the lure of the majors was well worth the ignominy of being labeled "scabs" by the Brothers.

Spalding also tried to snatch back National League defectors. Breach of contract suits were started in state courts, with lawyer Rodgers handling the legal work. Meanwhile newspapers loyal to the National League were fed propaganda linking the Players League with "hot headed anarchist" elements. And to neutralize press support for the players, Spalding threatened to withdraw advertising, a move that cowed some. Finally to secure a press voice in New York City, Spalding purchased the *Sporting Times* and installed the glib Oliver P. Caylor as its baseball editor.

Confident in the power of money, Spalding dangled it before players, some fourteen of whom took the bait. Included was pitcher John Clarkson, who was rumored to have taken $10,000 as his price for turning his coat. But Spalding failed to lure superstar "King" Kelly. Sorrowfully eyeing Spalding's proffered blank check, Kelly refused, saying: "My mother and father would never look at me again if I could prove a traitor to the boys." As expected, such enterprise sowed discord in Player ranks, moving the Brothers to concoct their own blacklist and to denounce turncoats and antiunionists as "scabs." [15]

But Spalding's legal attack failed miserably. On that front Ward staked his Columbia legal training on the theory that the courts would not sustain National contracts. After a series of defeats, the haggard Rodgers confessed that "in Pennsylvania our reserve clause will have to be rewritten, or it must disappear from all future contracts." And after losing in a New York Circuit Court of the United States, Rodgers quit the attack, having spent an estimated $15,000 in a losing cause.[16]

Beaten in the courts, the Nationals faced a standoff in the press war. Liberal editors like Richter, Al Spink, and Tim Murnane led a host of sportswriters backing the Players. However, newsmen had a real problem trying to cover the confused baseball season of 1890. Organizationally the two leagues were almost identical, as both had franchises in the same seven cities. Hence, on most days the two leagues played games at the same time, in the same town, but in separate parks. Yet strangely enough, Buffalo in the Players League and Cincinnati in the National, each with no opposition, proved to be the two most dismal financial failures. Elsewhere fans were forced to make a choice, with both leagues resorting to blatant lies about attendance figures. Sometimes physical force was used to persuade would be fans to make a proper choice.

Notwithstanding a bit of intimidation major league fans of 1890 never had it so good. Never in the history of major league baseball were tickets so easy to come by. It was a free loader's paradise. Both sides featured ladies' days and Spalding instituted an actor's day. President Charles Byrne of the National's Brooklyn team justified increasing the number of ladies' days at his park on the limp theory that fifty ladies were worth fifty cops in their inhibiting impact on rowdies. Of course, such gimmicks represented pathetic bids for support. In midseason Richter accused the Nationals of making a free show of baseball by depositing free tickets in saloons and barber shops.[17] And a *Herald* reporter's personal count suggested that New York teams were falsifying attendance figures. In 1891 something of a true picture emerged as the *Reach Guide* admitted that the Players had outdrawn the Nationals by 980,000 to 813,000.[18]

Other authorities agreed that the Nationals were worsted

at the gate. The objective Judge Cullom of New York kept a personal record of league profits and losses and stated that the Nationals lost over $300,000. But the Nationals were willing to take such a blow to win and its owners, remembering profitable days, were better equipped to hang on. Also the Nationals retained the services of good field managers like Anson of Chicago and Harry Wright of the Phillies. Such men by their charisma kept waverers in line and filled vacant gaps with shrewdly chosen rookies.[19]

The end of the 1890 season saw both sides exhausted. The National League Giants almost folded. Saved by the timely financial help of the Wagner brothers, traction company magnates from Philadelphia, was the Players' Philadelphia franchise. At this point the Nationals sustained another blow when the Players purchased the Nationals' Cincinnati franchise for $40,000. This setback plunged National leaders into gloom as it now looked as if another year of war was in the offing.

But the Players were reeling. True, they survived and even vitalized the game. More homers were hit by Players' teams thanks to the lengthened pitching distance, and the Boston Players, managed, captained, and joshed along by the easygoing "King" Kelly, won the pennant, beating off determined opposition from Ward's "Wonders," as Ward's lightly regarded Brooklyn entry was dubbed. But elsewhere the Players League picture was gloomy. All season long backers complained about a lack of discipline in the ranks. Many backers were further discouraged by losses. Brotherhood players also were surly over salary cuts and a lack of anticipated bonuses. It was enough to crush morale, and Ward was despondent over rumors of treason in Player ranks.

Not surprisingly recriminations dampened the annual meeting of the Players League in November. But the crushing blow fell when Pittsburg and New York resigned their memberships. With no replacements in sight, the league faced a shaky six club future in 1891. Then still another tremor came when the financial report showed only Boston making money; all others compiled a loss of $125,000, above and beyond the initial outlay for grounds and equipment. The report touched off a panic. Investors rushed to unload holdings and players sought to return to their old National masters.[20]

The streams of refugees were warmly welcomed by Spalding, who could afford to be magnanimous in victory. Rebel players were assured of no purges; even Ward was to be welcomed back. Thus, the final capitulation came in January 1891 when the Boston Players sold out to Spalding at a loss. After that surrender, Ward, Richter, and a few saddened financiers held a wake for the league at Nick Engel's in New York. Ward's cynical toast, "Pass the wine around, the League is dead, long live the League," caught the spirit of the moment. Richter took a brighter view: "Base Ball will live forever. Here's to the game and to its glorious future." [21]

Defeat meant renewed peonage for players as the dreaded salary limit became a reality. This occurred in 1892 after the National forces crushed the Association in 1891 and completed their monopoly of major league baseball. For the rest of the decade of the nineties major league baseball was dominated by a single twelve-club major league, the "big league" as it came to be called.

As for the reserve clause, it lived on without challenge. Indeed, players gloomily accepted the device as a "legal sin," conceding its necessity for the peculiar problems of baseball promotion. Ward said as much when he wrote in 1896:

> The sum and substance of the whole thing is that a baseball player must recognize the fact that baseball is a business, not simply a sport. It is not a Summer snap, but a business in which capital is invested. A player is not a sporting man. He is hired to do certain work, and do it well. . . . The amount of salary depends entirely upon the way he does his work, and it is for his own interest to keep himself in the best of condition, and study how to get the best results.[22]

NOTES

1. L. A. Wilder, "Baseball and the Law," *Case and Comment: The Lawyer's Magazine*, Vol. 19 (Aug. 1912), 153. Also, John W. Stayton, "Baseball Jurisprudence," *American Law Review*, Vol. 44 (May–June 1910), 380–81.

2. *New York Clipper*, Feb 14, 1885.

3. *Sporting Life*, Aug. 25, 1888. John M. Ward, *Baseball: How to Become a Player* (Philadelphia: Athletic, 1888).

4. *Sporting Life*, May 27, 1885; July 27, 1887; Oct. 19, 1887. *Sporting News*, May 10, 1890. *New York Clipper*, April 6, 1889.

5. *Sporting Life*, Oct. 19, 1887. *Sporting Life Official Guide, 1891*, p. 28. *The Players National League Official Guide for 1890*, pp. 6–10.

6. *Players Guide 1890*, p. 28. *Sporting News*, Dec. 31, 1886. *Sporting Life*, April 5, 1893.

7. *Sporting News*, Dec. 31, 1886.

8. *Sporting Life*, April 5, 1890.

9. J. M. Ward, "Is the Baseball Player a Chattel?" *Lippincott's Magazine*, Vol. 40 (Aug. 1887), 310–19. See also U.S. Congress, House Subcommittee on the Study of Monopoly Power, *Organized Baseball*, 82nd Cong., 2nd session, 1952.

10. *Players Guide 1890*, pp. 3–6. *New York Clipper*, Nov. 26, 1887; Dec. 3, 1887.

11. *Sporting Life*, Nov. 28, 1888; Dec. 5, 1888; Dec. 26, 1888; March 17, 1889.

12. *Players Guide 1890*, pp. 3–6. *Sporting Life Guide, 1891*, pp. 73–120.

13. *Sporting Life*, Nov. 13, 1889. *Players Guide 1890*, pp. 3–6.

14. *Players Guide 1890*, p. 106. *New York Clipper*, Dec. 28, 1889.

15. *Sporting Life*, Nov. 20, 1889; Dec. 25, 1889. *New York Clipper*, Nov. 23, 1889, Nov. 30, 1889. *Sporting News*, July 19, 1890.

16. Stayton, "Baseball Jurisprudence," pp. 380–85. *Boston Daily Globe*, April 7, 1890.

17. *Sporting Life*, July 5, 1890; Aug. 9, 1890. *Boston Daily Globe*, July 14, 1890; Aug. 9, 1890.

18. *Reach Guide, 1891*.

19. *Boston Daily Globe*, Aug. 21, 1890. *Sporting News*, Oct. 11, 1890.

20. *New York Clipper*, Oct. 11, 1890. *Sporting Life*, Nov. 29, 1890; Jan. 3, 1891.

21. *Sporting Life*, Jan. 24, 1890.

22. *New York Clipper*, Dec. 26, 1896.

Index

217